The
Hugging
Army

The Hugging Army

An Experience in Connection

Vanessa L. White Fernandes

THE HUGGING ARMY
AN EXPERIENCE IN CONNECTION

The views expressed in this work are solely those of the author
and do not necessarily reflect the views of the publisher, and the
publisher hereby disclaims any responsibility for them.

iUniverse books may be ordered through booksellers or by contacting:

iUniverse
1663 Liberty Drive
Bloomington, IN 47403
www.iuniverse.com
1-800-Authors (1-800-288-4677)

ISBN: 978-1-5320-4775-6 (sc)
ISBN: 978-1-5320-4776-3 (e)

Library of Congress Control Number: 2018904760

Print information available on the last page.

iUniverse rev. date: 04/20/2018

To Diane Michelle Fernandes, forever my soul sister. The dream of your heart put to the page through me. I am forever loving you.

Preface

This book is about a journey, one that I am still on. There is no final destination. It is a journey to self-love, to fully accepting and honoring who I am. The path is not always straight, smooth, or clear, yet it is always precisely where I need to be. I had no idea that hugging complete strangers would be such a catalyst in my awakening. And to this day, with every hugging experience, I understand and love myself and others more deeply and more authentically. For me, loving and accepting myself more fully is the key to loving and accepting others just as they are. Each hug, each interaction, is an opportunity to see my connection, my sameness. I am eternally grateful for each of those opportunities and the ones I know are to come.

Acknowledgments

There are so many people who have gently and lovingly helped in supporting this beautiful dream of connection. First, I want to thank my wife, Brenda, and my son, Jace. You have both provided unending support and enthusiasm for the Hugging Army and for my travels and adventures. Thank you for also being my devoted hugging partners. I love you both eternally. Zoe', thank you for supporting my writing, and moving out of your comfort zone to hug with me. I love you.

I also want to thank my mom and dad, my sisters, my brother, and my extended family, friends, and community for cheering me on, offering encouragement, and following me in my hugging pursuits.

In addition, a large part of what makes the Hugging Army is the army itself. Thank you to all who have joined the ranks so far, which includes Stacy, Missy, Grace, Heidi, Ivala, Lindsay, Jennifer, Ean, Rachel, Amie, Denise, Aubrey, Mary, Catherine, Becca, Nancy, Lindsey, Kelsey, Elise, and Tim—and those yet to join our team.

I also need to thank the various teachers in my life who, through books, lectures, and videos, have reminded me of the power of presence, the need for forgiveness, and the importance of inner peace.

Finally, I extend my deepest gratitude to the hundreds of strangers I have hugged and connected with over the years. I appreciate your willingness to reach across the human divide.

Introduction

My vision for the Hugging Army started in the early summer of 2015, but the foundation had been laid many years before that. Since the first time I stood on a busy sidewalk in June, it has continued to open up, change, grow, and manifest in ways I could have never anticipated. The deepest part of what I now learn and experience with every hug is how much I have to still learn about human beings, fear, connection, and what we need versus what we give to ourselves. It is a humbling experience to both hug another person and to have them decline a hug. It is eye-opening for me to share a deep, long exchange with another person and to have a high five from someone who is afraid to be touched by hugging. I learn more and more about what I am really made of, which is what we are all made of, ultimately. And I remember how fulfilling this offering has come to be for me. My wish for you, the reader, is that you will find a place in you that is willing to experience another way of seeing, especially if you are scared to do so or if you believe that things can never change. My hope is that you are able to see that we are all connected and you are never alone.

1

The Beginning

I always wanted to change the world, ever since I was a small child. To me, that meant to ease the suffering of others. As I grew older, it also came to mean showing people a preferred way of being. I came to see myself as someone with knowledge that a suffering person did not possess. There was compassion there—and a level of arrogance as well. By viewing others and myself in this way, I was able to detach myself from my sameness with that person, by seeing myself as wiser or as having the answers that they did not. I was living out, in part, the definition of a social worker. What I have learned instead is that I don't have to change others; I simply have to be different, or rather be my truest self in the world, and the change will take care of itself. Hugging strangers has taught me many valuable lessons in this way.

I didn't plan to be sort of obsessed with hugging people, complete strangers to me, on various city streets in my community or in other parts of the country. It is taking me in directions that I don't know I would have anticipated. And, like every great story, it starts at what feels like a beginning.

It was in the summer of 2013, and my partner, later to become my wife, wanted to take me to see Amma, also known by many as the Hugging Saint. I knew very little about Amma, beyond what my partner, Brenda, had told me of her, but what I did know was that she had hugged hundreds of thousands of people, all around the world, so far in her lifetime. In addition to her charitable works, she also offered hugs to anyone who waited to see her. I found that curious and somewhat strange. Now, up to that time in my life, I had always been a physically open person, often offering a hug and enjoying them when I received them from others. Even though I was not sure what to expect, I wanted to go.

We drove to New York City where Amma was going to be for part of her North American tour. Brenda forewarned me that hundreds of people would most likely be coming to see Amma while she was in New York—that it would be a large event and that we would most likely be waiting a lot of the time. That was no exaggeration; when we arrived, there were already dozens of people in a line, four or five people across, in a long corridor. The doors for entry were not even open yet, so we waited for an hour for that to happen. Next, we entered a large auditorium, and as we did, each person was given their number in line, a line that was hundreds of people long already. As we entered the auditorium, there were rows of chairs assembled, and on the open floor were dozens of vendors selling food, clothing, oils, and other items. As of eleven o'clock that morning, we would have hours to wait before we would get our hug.

Throughout the auditorium, there were large television screens on which to watch the events that were unfolding on a large stage at the front of the room. As the line moved along, we could move to different areas of chairs to be closer to the stage. The way that the schedule was going, we would not be hugging Amma until eleven or so that night. We still had a two-hour drive out of the city to get home after that, and we both had to work the next day. I wasn't even sure if I wanted to hug her. I mean, I love hugs, but this seemed almost too intense. And there was a part of me that was skeptical, that it wasn't a genuine offering.

Then I started to watch Amma giving hugs to people. On a screen, larger than life, I watched her hug people, one by one, as they came to her. She sat on the stage in an overstuffed chair, close to the floor. In order to hug her, you had to get down on your knees and kneel in front of the chair in which she was sitting. She hugged women, children, people with physical limitations, couples. As I sat and watched her hug one human being after another, I was so deeply moved that I could not stop crying. She wrapped her arms around each person so lovingly and held and rocked them from her chair. It was a deeply moving experience for me to witness. After watching her hug many other people, I knew that I did not want to leave that building without being hugged by her. And yet I also knew that it would be hours until we had our turn.

Brenda mentioned to one of her staff managing the line that we had driven a long way to see Amma and had a long drive home afterward. He was able to kindly move us up in the line so that we only had a short wait until we would be able to hug her. I was so excited. As we moved closer to the stage, I felt so inspired and fortunate to be able to experience this. There were several staff around, directing us regarding what we needed to do. As we went up on the stage, we would prepare to hug her by kneeling down. If we had any offerings for her, or any items that we wanted her to bless, we could also give those to the staff. I had purchased a necklace, carved from coconut shell, that I wanted her to bless for me. It was a lotus flower.

As it became my turn, staff guided me to Amma, directly in front of her chair. She immediately pulled me to her breast and held me strong and close. She rocked back and forth with me in her arms and was saying something in my ear that was another language and that I did not understand, but it seemed like a blessing. My heart felt like it had

3

burst open in that moment. I don't believe that, to that point, I had ever received such a deep, loving embrace from anyone in my life.

I felt forever changed after that somehow, like something in me that had been closed off was opened up again. It would take another circumstance to come along, courtesy of the internet, for me to fully realize what was to come next.

It was about a year later when I was browsing online that I came across a video of a man in Istanbul, Turkey. The video, which was about five minutes long, showed him standing in a congested area of the city with his arms wide open, a blindfold on, and a sign at his feet that read "I trust you, do you trust me? Hug me." I watched it in its entirety. Initially, people walked by him as he stood there, and then more and more people walked into his open arms and hugged him. A crowd of people stood around him as others hugged him. I watched it a few times, and every time, I felt a lump in my throat and was moved to tears. Something about that social experiment, that level of vulnerability and trust, really spoke to me. I wanted to show people they could trust me; I wanted to help others to not feel so scared.

I decided to try this same type of experiment here in my home city. It was the middle of winter when I saw the video, so I waited until the weather got warmer. I planned to conduct my version of it in June, on the first Friday of the month. Here, where I live, the first Friday of every month is a celebration of local art and music in our downtown. Art galleries are bustling with new shows, musicians play live on the sidewalks, and the streets are teeming with life. It seemed like the ideal time to offer free hugs. I created a sign similar to the one in the video. On a large board, it read: "I trust you, do you trust me? How about a hug?" Brenda agreed to come along with me to support me and to take photographs of the experience. What happened next was another indication that I was onto something profound and life changing.

2

How about a Hug?

It was the first weekend in June 2015, and First Friday was in full swing in the downtown area. The air was warm, and it was a beautiful evening. Summer was on her way, and the city was bustling. I was excited for this new experience—and scared at the same time. There I was, standing on the sidewalk, a blindfold over my eyes and a sign that invited people to hug me. Having Brenda nearby helped me to feel less vulnerable. I felt inspired to stand with my arms wide open, thinking that people would feel more welcomed. I stood for a few minutes, listening to the traffic and the people walking by. I was curious about what would happen, knowing that what I was doing was potentially dangerous. I mean, the most vulnerable part of my body was exposed, my heart, yet I knew it would be okay. My arms got tired from holding them up, so I put them down every few minutes and then opened them up again.

After about fifteen minutes, I felt someone come into my arms, very gently, and I started to wrap my arms around their body. They didn't say a word, but I could hear what seemed like a man's voice, softly giggling. Without my sense of sight, it was difficult for me to navigate where to wrap my arms. Was this an arm? An elbow? As I was figuring it out, I felt a small, fuzzy head. I started to cry.

"Honey, it's a baby!" I shouted out. I was hugging a small, sweet baby who had been put into my arms by her father. I could hardly believe that my first hug ever was a small child. It felt like the epitome of trust and love in that small moment.

I knew that whatever came next would be just as special. It was like part of me had cracked open through the experience, and I was doing precisely what I was meant to do that evening—offering hugs. Some of the hugs were brief, and others were long, tight, and firm. Most people hugged me without saying a word. In fact, a few of my friends came by that evening for a hug and never told me that they were there; only when I saw their photo later did I realize I had hugged them. I stood there for ninety minutes that evening and hugged about seventy-five people.

There were many memorable hugs that I would later recall as I looked at the photographs. One small child came and hugged me twice that evening, wrapping her little body around the lower part of my body. My roommate from college, who was never a physically affectionate person, came and hugged me. I would have never recognized her by her hug; it wasn't until I saw her picture later on that I realized she had been there. It was powerful and magical. One woman wearing a burka

7

cried in my arms, telling me the story of her unhappy life, and then her daughter hugged me next, thanking me for my offering.

One hug stood out from the rest that evening. I had been standing on the sidewalk for about an hour and had several hugs offered to me. Most people were soft and slow in their approach as they came in for a hug, briefly touching my hand or arm to let me know they were there, and then hugging me. However, this person came directly into my arms, with no warning at all. They wrapped both arms around me, put their head on my shoulder, and hugged firmly. I felt a relaxation into my arms, unlike any hug I had experienced that evening. It was firm and solid yet not too tight. After about twenty seconds, which is a long time when you're hugging someone, I started to release my hold on the person, and they held on even tighter, not yet ready to release. Our hug was close to a minute in its entirety, and then they let go and left. It was the most present and powerful hug of that evening. When I looked at the pictures later, I saw that the person appeared to be male. I couldn't see his face but wondered if we had since passed each other on the street. His hug has stayed with me ever since that night.

As the evening ended, I felt so energized and alive. In the days following the experience, I thought about what lessons I had learned. Connecting with so many people who previously had been strangers to me opened up my heart and presented so many possibilities of what could come next. I realized that I had shown vulnerability, standing there with my arms wide open to strangers, yet, by wearing a blindfold, I also had a barrier between me and the people I was hugging. For me, the experience was one of offering trust and asking for trust in return, but there was more to it than that. I also realized that it was an experience in present-moment awareness, the knowing that *this moment is all I have*. As I stood there, not knowing what would happen, being in the moment helped me to let go of expectations of what might happen and let the events unfold naturally. When I looked at the photographs that captured the hugs, I also realized that it seemed I was able to offer to others that which they needed, even if they may not have fully realized that at the time.

After that first hugging experience, I was busy planning for our wedding, which was coming up that summer. We got married in July and had an amazing honeymoon. I continued to think about my experience with hugging others and felt compelled to plan another experience. However, in my understanding of all that I had been seeking in it and all that I had learned through the experience, I wanted to conduct it somewhat differently.

By wearing a blindfold, I had put a barrier between me and the other person. It gave a sense of comfort and safety in that neither of us had to be seen. However, with this new experience, I wanted to take the mask off. I wanted to look at people eye to eye, and I wanted others to know that I saw them as they were. I decided that my sign would read, "I see your humanity, do you see mine?" I assumed that people would welcome hugs that were offered by someone who was seeing them as they were. And although I tried not to have expectations for how it would unfold, I wanted to get as many hugs as possible.

Again I chose a First Friday, which also happened to be the opening night of a large Italian festival in the downtown area of the city. The evening was amazing—warm and full of light. I stood in the same spot as before, my arms wide open, my sign near me, and Brenda standing by to take photographs. Right from the start, the sensation was much different because I soon realized I would be able to see the people who would come for a hug and those who would not. I even found myself making assumptions about who would want hugs from me (people who knew me, people who were there for the festival) and people who would not (people from the local art community). Even though I realized that these were just assumptions, I found myself taken in by the stories in my mind.

I waited to see what would unfold. Within a few minutes, a young person came up to me. I had seen her in the photographs from my previous hugging experience, but she hadn't come to me for a hug. She had her arms wide open this time, coming for one. It was really beautiful and fun to see the smile of recognition and openness on her face.

Being eye to eye with people, seeing their humanness, was a real gift to me. There were so many beautiful hugs that night. I did not know most of the people who came by that evening, yet they came to me with full, open arms, and the hugs were warm, long, and firm. It was truly incredible. One woman appeared to be homeless, with all her belongings on her back and on the back of her dog. When I asked her if she would like a hug, she said to me, "I probably smell. You don't want to hug me." I told her I didn't care and hugged her. It was lovely. At the very end of the evening, I was getting ready to leave, and I saw an older woman with a walker coming toward me. I asked her, "Are you coming for me?" With a big smile, she said, "Yes!" I gave her and her partner two deep hugs. I was floating on a cloud.

I learned a lot about myself again that evening. Even though I had believed I would feel accepting and open about people who did not wish to be hugged, in reality, that wasn't the case. I took it personally when someone walked by and didn't want a hug. Intellectually, I understood some of the reasons a person might not be comfortable with hugs. At the same time, I saw what I was offering as a genuine gift that everyone *should* want. At times, this created a barrier to the experience and to staying present, because I was more focused on the people who did not want a hug than those who did. However, it eased over the course of the evening, and the realization that I had been taking it personally was a deep lesson that stayed with me as I continued to offer hugs.

3

Finding the Fringe

I knew that even though hugging remained part of my everyday world, with the people in it, something was shifting in me with the offering of hugs to strangers, although I was still not fully clear what that was. I met a friend who also liked to offer hugs to others and carried a Free Hugs sign with her in her car. We started to offer hugs together at various locations, such as art events and holiday celebrations. It felt fun to have someone who shared this desire with me, and I appreciated not always being alone as I offered hugs to others. At the same time, I wanted to be able to share these experiences with people on a larger scale, to talk about why I believed hugs were so important and for everyone. To me, hugs are important because they create connection between people; they can reduce heart rate and respiration; they help us to get present to our breath; they remind us that we are not alone; they help to heal us from our emotional pain; and so much more! I wasn't really clear about what that would look like, although I was writing frequently about hugs and my hugging experiences on my blog.

Then I found out about an arts and music festival in my city, the Scranton Fringe Festival. It's four days of shows and performances in comedy, music, performing arts, theatre, storytelling, and visual arts. I wasn't sure that what I wanted to talk about would be considered art or welcomed in such a festival. I held a belief that I was not a real artist, so might not fit into the format. I realized that was merely self-doubt and decided to go ahead and apply anyway.

When I first put in my application, my vision of the show was that I would show photographs of my hugging experiences as I told stories. I also wanted to talk about what I learned about myself as I continued offering hugs, about the benefits of hugs, and the need for deep human connection. I called the show "I Want YOU to join the Hugging Army." Since it felt like a movement of sorts, I wanted it to be a call to arms, so to speak.

I received my acceptance to the Fringe Festival just a few weeks after I applied. I was thrilled—and scared. Even though I knew that I was more than capable of creating a show that would inspire others, my self-doubt was present. As soon as I was accepted, I immediately wanted to change the name of the show, thinking that the Hugging Army sounded aggressive or too fierce. It was too late to change the name, so I had to work with it. It ended up being the greatest afterthought in regard to the project.

I really thought about and began to understand why it felt like an army. To me, Hugging Army was the perfect name because it reminded me that talking to others about human connection and the healing power of hugs felt like starting a revolution. I knew of and had experienced many people who stated that they did not like to be touched, or for whom touch was hurtful in some way. However, I believed that touch is how to heal, even if we have been hurt. And I knew that the message of connection and healing would not just be me passing it on; it would be an invitation to anyone who felt ready to join me. I would need a host of supports, volunteers, or "troops" to assist in the movement.

So I started putting together what my show would actually look like. I gathered all the photographs that had been taken over the previous year of my hugging experiences and did a bit of research about the nature of hugs, the benefits of hugs, the lack of human connection, and present-moment awareness and mindfulness. The show felt like it would be a story and also a testament to how things are, in contrast to how I thought they should be. I would be ending the show by teaching those in the audience how to give and receive a deep, mindful hug. I also gathered volunteers to help with the show and the offering of hugs. I had quite a few friends and loved ones by my side!

I was given two show times, both at a hotel venue in downtown Scranton. I had a list of songs to play prior to the show and at the end as we were giving hugs to one another. I did a lot of advertising, putting out postcards for the show and posting about it often on social media. Even though I wasn't sure how many people would attend my show, I wanted to manifest a great turnout.

The Scranton Fringe Festival was an amazing experience. I made many new friends, some who lived there and others who came from out of town. I realized that I fit right in with the artists and musicians of the local area. People were supportive and encouraging, and I had audiences for both of my shows. Even though some people who attended weren't sure what the show was all about, they wanted to check it out.

Since the pictures tell such a sweet story about my hugging experiences, they were an essential and beautiful part of the show. I told the stories of my first hug with the baby; about the young person who hugged me for a full minute; and about the homeless woman. I talked about the people who did not hug me, about all that I learned about myself through my experiences. I wanted to help people to understand our lack of connection—and how we crave it at the same time.

From my perspective, at one time or another we all feel alone on this journey we call life. We feel scared, and we are trying to navigate a chaotic world that we exist in. I believe that everyone wants connection, even though we lack it in our lives at times. I also believe that we want to remember our own innocence, yet many factors and things that we learn along the way block our vision. We all are born innocent, full of truth, light, and love.

It is easy to see the innocence of a baby, or any new life form for that matter, be it a puppy, kitty, or human. When we look deeply into their eyes and watch how they play and learn about their world, we see the magic and wonder. We love that these new beings are so wild, so free with how they learn and what they do in their world. We all start out that way. But then we begin to learn from others what is expected of us, what is right and wrong, what is proper and what is not. We start to learn that it is not okay to be wild and free and that we should think and believe in a certain way. We become afraid to be ourselves.

As a result, we learn to create a certain image of who we are supposed to be, and then we want that image to be perfect. When we don't live up to the image we have created, as a result of what we have been taught, we criticize and demean ourselves for not being perfect.

We judge not only ourselves but also others when they are not perfect in our eyes, based on what it is we have learned. We also learn to pretend to be something we are not, so that we can maintain this level of perfection. We eventually punish ourselves, and those around us, for not meeting that perfection. We do this by hurting ourselves and others with words and thoughts that are judgmental about how less than perfect we all are. We all then become so hurt that we don't want to communicate with others, and we become afraid to trust others. Ultimately, we become people who are socialized to be separate from one another, to communicate through text and social media, and to live in fear of deeply connecting with others.

What I find most upsetting and upside down about this process is that, ultimately, we fear connection at the same time that we deeply crave having it with one another. Physical touch is an essential part of that. Newborn babies who are not held consistently fail to thrive in the world and have long-standing physical and emotional problems. As human beings, we are meant to be held and physically nurtured by one another. Just think of how much we want to hold babies and young children, and they love being held in return. Yet, as we age, we forget how important that it is to us and our well-being.

Through my show at the Fringe Festival, I invited people to forget what they had learned in their lives and to be radical and consider another way to look at relationships and human connection. Although I believe that most humans remember what the real truth is about connection and physical touch, we have forgotten it over time.

I taught people what a deep, mindful hug was and how to give and receive one. A mindful hug is a simple yet powerful gesture, because what it brings to the interaction is pure, deep presence and love. When we are deeply aware of the present moment, we can have deeper human connections, and as our human connections deepen, we can be more present in the moment. They work in synchronicity with one another. In addition, hugs are known to improve mood, lower blood pressure, and restore balance to our bodies and minds. I also spoke about how mindful hugging helps us to remember that we are not alone and that we are all connected.

We spent the last fifteen minutes of both shows sharing hugs with one another. The hugs were deep, mindful hugs that lasted for three full breaths. There was so much love and presence in the room. Many people, including myself, were crying tears of deep longing and oneness. It was pure beauty.

After the Fringe Festival ended, I was on a high for days. I felt like I had fulfilled one of my dreams, to feel inspired by something and to be able to share that with others and deepen their understanding and their sense of connection to one another. I knew that somehow I had to keep the momentum going with my free hugs and talking about them. I started hearing about how expansive Fringe Festivals were all over the world, including here in the United States. Cities all over the country were having festivals just like the one in Scranton. I applied for and was accepted to do the show in the Pittsburgh Fringe Festival in April 2017.

4

The Hug Bug Tour

With months to go before the next official show, I felt like I wanted to do something with the Hugging Army that was connected to my 1998 VW Beetle, the Hug Bug. I felt inspired and compelled to plan for some sort of trip that would enable me to offer hugs in all different areas of the country, although I didn't know practically or creatively what that would look like. After conducting the Hugging Army show at Scranton Fringe and planning for Pittsburgh Fringe, I believed that the show was solid enough that other groups and organizations would be interested in hearing my stories and seeing my photographs.

One day, I came up with the idea of doing what came to be called the Hug Bug Tour. The vision was simple: go to cities, offer free hugs on the street, and then conduct a presentation of the Hugging Army at a local church or other public venue. It would be offered free of charge, and I would stay with friends who lived in those local areas, friends I had made over the years through blogging and having an online presence. After considering various dates, I decided to go in the first week of June 2017.

I reached out to my many friends and family members in various areas, and all of them were excited and hopeful that the Hugging Army would be well received in their area. They also were more than gracious to have me stay with them during my travels. So, I began the work of planning where I would go during what would be ten days on the road.

The details of planning such an endeavor seemed complex, but I found myself thoroughly enjoying the process. My first confirmation for talking about the Hugging Army was in Fort Payne, Alabama, my farthest point south. It was coordinated by a friend of mine, Kristy. I had met Kristy and her daughter, Emily, on the street in Asheville, North Carolina, offering hugs as my wife played music. We had stayed in touch, and she was a member of a long-standing meditation group that wanted to host my discussion.

A few weeks later, I confirmed that I would be speaking at a Metropolitan Community Church in Charleston, South Carolina, coordinated by my friend Julie, who lived there. However, I was not having success at the other venues I hoped to visit. I was having a difficult time finding spaces that wanted to host me to talk about my experiences. I was having trouble putting into words, in a consistent and concise way, what my mission and purpose were. In February 2017, I began to get discouraged. I wanted to take this trip, and I wanted to talk about hugging to whomever would listen. Yet the details were not falling into place in the way of my expectations.

I decided, then and there, that this trip would occur, with or without venues at every stop to talk to people. I would simply show up in a city, offer free hugs, and document my experiences. I finalized my destinations and reached out to friends about where I would stay. My itinerary as I planned it looked something like this:

Saturday: Punxsutawney, PA
Sunday: Asheville, NC
Monday: Raleigh, NC
Tuesday: Charleston, SC
Wednesday: Fort Payne, AL
Thursday: Charlotte, NC
Friday: Greensboro, NC
Saturday: Hurdle Mills, NC
Sunday: Washington, DC

It was a tall order. I would be driving for several hours each day, some days a few hundred miles. I also noticed that I had many stops planned in North Carolina. With Asheville being one of my favorite cities, I had a deep affection for the state. I got busy formalizing my plans for the trip.

I was also preparing for my show at the Pittsburgh Fringe Festival in early April. I would be staying with my son, Jace, who lived an hour or so from the city, and he was going to assist me with the show as well. The venue in Pittsburgh was a bit different, in that it was the sitting area in a home that served as a bed-and-breakfast for travelers. I liked the idea of the venue but became concerned about the need for technology for my show. I decided that instead of having a collage of pictures shown through a projector, I would use my favorite photographs from my experiences and make them into storyboards. That way, not only would I be free of any technology needs, but I could also connect with my audience in a more personal way. At first, I wasn't enthusiastic about changing the format of my photographs; change can be difficult for me to embrace. However, I made the decision and trusted that it would be a positive change for the show.

The decision was a good one. The shows at Pittsburgh Fringe were a complete success. The setting was intimate, and the stories felt vital and alive. The poster boards were a brilliant way to bring the stories to life with my audience that was sitting just a few feet from me. The audience was captivated by the words, and the pictures made them real. At the end of both shows, we shared deep, mindful hugs with one another and talked about the importance of connection. To be able to again have that experience with a group of strangers, and in addition, to have my son assisting me, was a dream come true. The more I gave free hugs and talked about it, the more I knew that it was what I was meant to be doing.

5

Heading South

After the Pittsburgh Fringe Festival, I started documenting my travels and experiences more formally by keeping a journal. My next trip was to Lexington, Kentucky, to visit and offer hugs at the University of Kentucky. My son's girlfriend was a student there, and he was considering a transfer there in the fall. I was excited to see the state of Kentucky again. I had been there once before and loved it. I was also excited to see how free hugs would be received there. One of the most interesting parts of traveling and giving free hugs is my tendency to assume how receptive people will be, given a certain age range or geographical area. No matter what assumptions I start out with, they always get busted—every single time.

On my way to western Pennsylvania to pick up my son, I was filled with wonder again about my desire to offer free hugs to others. Why did traveling away from home and holding up a sign, or wearing one, for hours appeal to me? What was in it for me? What was I hoping to gain, accomplish, or prove? What I came to realize more deeply was that it had evolved into an act that was an offering to the world around me. The offering was one of possibility. On most days, in most situations, I feel certain that I am one with all beings and that we all come from the same source. However, I am not sure that most humans feel that sense of certainty, because there is so much fear. Fear appears in various forms within each of us. Ultimately, the fear that lives in all of us is a fear of death—death of the physical body, death of the illusion of life, death of an idea or concept. So, instead of preaching to others in a way that has the conviction of certainty, and at times arrogance, I believe I am offering to others the possibility of what may exist, a different way to look at things. It is possible that connection and love exist in a mad world.

I feel both a sense of excitement and a sense of nervousness when I strike out on a new hugging adventure. It's the anticipation and fear that live in me. But when I remember to come back to the present moment, as often as possible, I let go of both excitement and nervousness and just let things unfold beautifully. And it always does just that.

As I traveled to Punxsutawney on Interstate 80, the first leg of my journey to Kentucky, a passenger in a pickup truck passing by my Hug Bug, with the Free Hugs sign in the back window, put his whole upper body out of his window, arms outstretched toward me. As he made eye contact with me and I gave him an embrace from behind the wheel, he broke out in the most amazing, beautiful smile! I was enjoying the journey from the very beginning. For months, I had in the back window of my car a Free Hugs sign displayed. It was propped up just enough that people could see what it said. There had been many responses to that sign. Some people gave me a thumbs-up, an air hug, a peace sign, or a wave. Some people just smiled and nodded. I have seen many people pull up close enough to take a picture on their cell phone. In a way, it has been a sort of social experiment to see how people respond.

When we arrived in Kentucky, we walked around the campus and saw the sites. I wore one of my Hugging Army T-shirts, which read "Hug Some One" on the back. We then decided to go shopping at a local mall, and I decided I would stand in the mall and offer free hugs while we were there. My son and his girlfriend decided to join me. Wearing the T-shirts and holding signs, we stood together in the center of the mall. It was a busy Saturday, and many people were walking by.

Eye contact is a key element for me when offering hugs. In the past, I have had a difficult time maintaining eye contact with people during conversations or when passing someone on the street. I felt self-conscious and vulnerable when I met eyes with someone. Yet I know now that it is essential to connecting with another person. As my son, his girlfriend, and I stood in the mall, offering hugs to people who walked by, I made eye contact with my fellow humans as often as possible. Just my offering of a smile and a nod was enough for some people and definitely enough for me. Exchanging a smile with a stranger, whether or not we ever connect physically, is beautiful and heartwarming.

During our time there, one woman sent her small daughter over to me, and she came in for a one-armed side hug. I love it when parents send their young children over or bring them to me as I am hugging, because it feels like the ultimate trust. Later on, a young person came up to my son from behind, grabbed him around the shoulders in a hug, and then came back around twice, for another hug and to give us all candy. My son, after having offered hugs with me in the past, finds it as addictive and fulfilling as I do. His girlfriend was a bit nervous at first, as she had never done it before. However, once people started hugging her, she wanted more of it and kept holding the sign and calling it in.

During my hugging experiences, people sometimes ask what it's all about and why I'm doing it. However, more often than not, people thank me for the hug, and many state that they really needed one that day. There are also people who are afraid to connect in that way. After about an hour at the mall, a security guard came by, telling us that we were not allowed to be there without permission from the management, and before I could ask him how to do that, he walked away. He appeared irritated and edgy as he confronted us. We took our stuff and started walking around the mall, our T-shirts still on and carrying our signs. Some people came to us for hugs and took pictures. Whether standing in one spot or walking around, we got to spread the connection as far as possible.

When we returned to the university campus, we walked around town a bit. We were still carrying our signs. One person asked me about the sign and then proceeded to tell me that she had issues with her back and could not give or receive hugs. There were many people who wanted to get hugs as well. One group of people came up to us full of excitement to give and receive hugs. One of them even offered us freshly baked cookies as a thank-you gesture.

6

The Transformation Begins

In giving free hugs, I get to offer people something that they may not realize they needed, something surprising to them in a world where they might feel overwhelmed and unseen. And I don't have to do anything really. I'm just being—standing in my light, being myself, and letting that light shine through for others to see. It is an invitation for love—to come in if they desire, or to pass by.

My offering of hugs continues to evolve and change as I give them. When I first put on a blindfold and stood with my sign on the street, I wanted to prove something to others. I wanted to prove to other people they could trust me; in a world that is chaotic and violent, I was willing to be vulnerable, without my sight, to "prove" that they could trust me. I saw people as hurting and fed up with the world, needing what I had to offer. I saw people as not being able to take care of themselves, and although I told myself that it was coming from a space within me of compassion, I actually was seeing myself as their hero, and them in need of saving.

One of the things that I talk to my audiences about when discussing my hugging experiences is the growth, or expansion, of my humility. As a social worker for over thirty years, I have come to see myself as

26

indispensable to others. Not only in my work but also in my family, I have enjoyed having the role of the person who is there for everyone and whose skills and expertise are needed in any difficult situation. Again, even though I thought I was being compassionate, I didn't really see others as capable of solving their own problems. It was my own special version of arrogance.

When I anticipated going out on the road, traveling hundreds of miles to destinations, some of which I had never been to, I would get excited and scared. My fears around hugging were about being rejected or disappointed. I always seem to feel most vulnerable when I'm first standing, arms out, sign around my neck. Then I welcome into myself this quiet, peaceful sense of knowing—a knowing who I am and what I want. It allows my fears to dissipate, and I realize that I no longer care about whether people want hugs or not, and I am never disappointed. The experience is always magical and new. I bring nothing different to my hugging experiences than I do to any aspect of my life. It is all offered freely. I just have to say yes!

What keeps pulling me toward this? The part of me, or rather, the me that is my pure, true form. Not my identity or the part that I try to make into an identity. I feel it in the space in me for which there are no words that can accurately describe. It feels like a warm glow that begins in my chest, my heart chakra and radiates out from there. It has no origins in any religious belief or any philosophy. It has evolved on its own, purely based on that feeling, and my experience and evolution related to it. The less I put an expectation on it, the more pure and present the experience is realized.

Sometimes when I think about what I'm offering through hugs, I use different words, such as healing, awareness, love, and presence. And I do believe, in part, that is true. But the truer sense is that I am offering myself; what people take away from that is up to them. When I release them from the expectation of receiving something specific, I can allow it to be as it is and for the experience to simply expand into the space.

Through hugging other people, I have learned to more openly accept and literally embrace the humanness and innate perfection that exists in all of us. It has taught me that all living beings are worthy of love, affection, peace, and compassion. It reminds me that we are the same universally. It has humbled me to learn, and to continue to learn, that the more I judge myself, the more I will judge others as well. And that I don't have to save or fix anyone I meet. When I see others as no different from me, no separateness, I can offer true compassion. Compassion feels deeper and purer to me than empathy. Empathy, to me, is me having an understanding of your feelings. Compassion feels like an opening of my heart, opening my arms like wings and wrapping them around that person and their presence, whatever it is.

I continued to have some beautiful experiences with hugging, just in our own local area. My energy kept building when I thought about the Hug Bug Tour, so I was grateful for any additional experiences until I would be leaving. One evening, my wife and I went out to dinner at a small, local place. When we pulled up (I was driving the Hug Bug), patrons and workers were sitting outside smoking. As we said hello to them, one young person said, "I'll take a free hug." At first, I was confused about his statement; I didn't have my sign on. But I figured out that he had seen my Free Hugs sign in the back window of my car. He thanked us both for our hugs, saying that he had really needed them.

I also had opportunities, as I gave free hugs, to challenge some of my limiting beliefs and assumptions. As a social worker and someone who has worked in the field of mental health for over thirty years, I have met dozens of people with a mental health diagnosis. On occasion, when I would meet with people, adults and children, I would offer them a hug as a way to comfort or connect. At times, I would struggle with whether or not to offer it, having been instructed about boundaries and differences. I was asked by a friend if I would want to offer free hugs at a local community awareness walk that was being sponsored by the local chapter of the National Alliance on Mental Illness. It was a more beautiful experience than I could have imagined. Although I believed that I was pretty free of biases and stereotypes, I assumed that people at the walk, particularly those with a mental health diagnosis, might not be comfortable with being touched, or that I might not know how to respond if they were outwardly displaying "symptoms." All that disappeared the minute I simply opened my arms, with the sign around my neck. Many people that day welcomed my offering and interaction. I felt a deep, personal connection with each person I hugged that day. It was yet another reminder of the universal nature of us all, no matter what path we walk or what our experiences are. We each have our own set of struggles and suffering. And my own capacity for understanding and compassion is only ever one thought away.

I have continued to learn that there is nothing specific that I need to do in this world, to heal, help, or fix another person. I can see others as whole, capable, and worthy, just as they are, and then just offer what I do for whomever wishes to receive it. I didn't have to view myself as some sort of hero anymore, or as the expert who had to save everyone else. I understand now that there is no one to save.

I have embraced or adopted several identities in my life so far: mother, daughter, wife, sibling, social worker, friend, life coach. When I am standing with another human being, arms outstretched, wrapping ourselves around one another, all my identities dissolve. I am just a human being, spirit in human form, standing with another human being, another spirit in human form. It brings an intimacy that would not be present if I were attempting to look for the ways in which we are the same or different. It just allows us both to be.

I come back to my center of calm and peace quite often when I'm offering hugs. When I first begin, it can feel like chaos, like I'm in the middle of busyness, with people looking at me, and me feeling not quite sure of what I'm doing. I also believe at times that I am being judged and viewed as strange. For a few moments, I feel a sense of fear, like I should just run and hide, to be alone. Instead, I keep breathing deeply. I come back to my center by focusing on my breath, lightly closing my eyes, and remembering why I am there. What is my purpose? What feels most important to me?

The answer is always the same: peace. Sometimes it takes me a bit of time to get there. I know it is my true, ultimate desire. And no matter what is going on around me, I always get to choose it. I understand more deeply with every experience that the more present, open, and peaceful I am, the more the world welcomes and receives what I am offering.

Hugging strangers has also reminded me of the importance of having fun! Being spontaneous, open, smiling, and available. There is nothing like the bright openness of a human who comes into my arms and feeling the warmth and joy of a hug. A small child so ready to run to me or to give me a high five. The soft nature of my evolution with hugs allows me to be playful with it all, to not take it so seriously.

I have met people over the years who do not understand my hugging of strangers. Or they feel concerned about me traveling alone to different parts of the country. When I'm asked about that, I don't feel any sense of defending it within me anymore; I just feel at ease in my own truth of why I'm doing it. I believe that humans are inherently good, and most of the time, I see and understand the universal light that is in all of us. Sure, sometimes I get scared. My biggest fear, the only fear ultimately, is the fear of death. Yet I trust and know that what I'm doing feels good, and right, and true. So, I keep on doing what I'm doing.

7

Impermanence and the Present Moment

As I thought about traveling on my Hug Bug Tour or talked to others about it, I was filled with such a sense of excitement and purpose. I knew I was meant to be doing that in my life and that it was a genuine path for me to be walking. I knew more deeply than ever that shining my own light in the world in order to connect with others was the path, despite meeting so many people who were reluctant to show their true selves in the world on any consistent basis. I understood that the more authentic I was in the world, the more brilliant my light would emanate from me. It was less about becoming someone and more about being.

As my plans were getting finalized, I had no venues in mind or events planned. I would just be going to the city that I chose, and if there was no scheduled event planned for me, I would find a public spot to give hugs. I was learning to let go of any attachment to what I wanted the experience to be like. Even in those places where I had events planned, I had no idea what would actually happen.

There exists in me, still to this day, a part that always wants to be prepared and to know how things are going to turn out. What I have learned, however, is that the less that I am focused on my projected outcome, or expectation, the more magical the experience actually is. When I am not waiting for one particular outcome, everything that comes my way is a gift.

I also believe that being more in touch with my own mortality and the transient nature of all things has encouraged me to do everything possible to live a full, joyful life. The more often I stay present in the moment, and the more often I realize that I have no problems in this moment, the more I will savor the moment. It helps me to tap into my spontaneous, free nature. Yes, expectations always arise, and they were arising in the plans for my tour. Yet, the more often I come back to the present moment, the more fullness I experience in life. Presence allows me to be excited just to be myself in the world, without apology, and to be excited about others being themselves as well.

In addition, I know that the deepest lessons I have learned in my life have been learned with another person, in some form of relationship with them. In that exchange with another person, rather than in isolation, there are assumptions, biases, and judgments that get burned up, and new levels of understanding and connection are born. Even when relationships end, they make room for what new is coming next.

Knowing that I would be traveling for hundreds of miles every day, for ten days, all alone on the road, I thought a lot about what seemed to be the truth about the world. The world seems to be a place of violence and fear, and at times my own fears create obstacles for me around wanting to be out in it. Will I die? Will something go wrong? I know that these possibilities exist in the hours of every day, and I have been able to obtain wisdom that has helped me to stay safe. Or so I thought. In reality, anything can happen in any given moment, no matter how safe I believe myself to be. But I know that despite my impermanence, and despite my fears, living my life fully and authentically is all I can ever do. Be present, embrace the moment, and have plenty of adventures.

8

The Hug Bug Tour 2017 Begins

Two days before leaving on the Hug Bug Tour, I invited several friends to join me at a local restaurant to celebrate my trip and departure. We shared food, drink, and stories with one another. I was more excited than ever for the trip, and the night was magical. I talked about my inspiration, my mission, things that are deeply in my heart and soul, and to have so many lovely people around to support and honor that was deeply emotional. It reminded me that although I was embarking on something brand-new and unknown, ultimately I would be fully cared for. So many beautiful souls joined me that evening, including Brenda, Trish, Will, Kacie, Matt, Tim, Susan, Meira, Brian, Christine, Brittany, Mandy, Dana, Tom, Uta, Jeff, Lydia, Greg, and Jesse. By the end of the evening, my heart was overflowing with joy and gratitude.

On June 2, I began the journey that would change me in so many deep, profound ways. That day, I worked a full day from home, and in between calls, I packed up my belongings and loaded my car. I had planned out in my brain for weeks how I would set up items in my car so that what I needed would be within reach and everything would have its place. All day, I felt deep excitement, some fear, and a swell of deep emotion, knowing that I was being led in this next part of my life journey. I trusted that anything and everything that I required would be shown to me, provided for me, and given to me.

Even on the day of my departure, after letting go of expectations of what the trip would be like, I still had thoughts of wanting it to be a certain way. I wanted to reach a certain amount of people or be invited to more venues. The bigger part of me, however, still remembered that it wasn't even about how many hugs were given or people I encountered; it was about the adventure and beauty of every moment on the journey. Each hug, each exchange, each decline of an offered hug, and each night sleeping alone would bring so many lovely and necessary lessons for me.

I also knew that I wanted to document my trip as fully as possible, not only for myself but to share with others after the trip was over. Up to the day I left, so many people, known and unknown to me, were following my plans and supporting me from afar. Many of those people are fascinated by what I do; they themselves cannot envision being that vulnerable in the world, yet they think it's amazing that someone else would want to be. My local paper had written an amazing article about the Hug Bug Tour and included pictures of me with the Hug Bug and my Free Hugs sign. The excitement of seeing that in print was addictive. Yet, after it had been published for a day, I started to feel too vulnerable, like too much of me was out in the open for the world to see. I had an impulse to go into hiding and into my own shell.

Yet I realized that, to me, there is no such thing as being too vulnerable; I either choose to be vulnerable, and all that means, or I don't. And I had already found that the deepest joy, love, grief, pain, and lessons had come to me when I would literally stand with my arms wide open. It had already brought more to me than I could have ever imagined for myself.

9

Day 1: Scranton, PA, to Punxsutawney, PA—213 Miles

At the end of my workday, I was ready to get in my car and depart. My first evening would be spent in Punxsutawney with my son. I started the four-hour drive to his house. If you have never heard of Punxsutawney, which it took me months to spell correctly, it is the home of the groundhog Phil, who is relied upon every February to predict the last weeks of winter. It is a small, unassuming town, with storefronts and citizens who seem family oriented and faithful. My son had been living there for almost a year, and I wanted to make Punxy, as it is known there, my first stop. My son and I wanted to offer hugs together to kick off my tour. On the way there, during that first leg of the journey, I received a few beeps of car horns from my Free Hugs sign and one air hug from a car passenger while passing me, and when I stopped at a truck stop, two people actually asked me for a hug. I was off to an amazing start.

Day 2: Punxsutawney, PA, to Asheville,
NC (Part I)—350 miles

The following morning, which was Saturday, we had breakfast and then drove to the downtown area of Punxy to see what was happening. Things were moving, yet it was relatively quiet. My son, Jace, and I had been walking around town and had gotten a fair number of long glances and smiles from people driving by. We stepped into the groundhog souvenir shop, which was on the main street right in town. I wanted to purchase some postcards to send messages to my supporters and friends while I was on the tour. I found just the right ones and some really cool T-shirts as well for both of us. As we were checking out, the woman behind the counter said, after seeing us both holding Free Hugs signs, "Okay, I have to ask …" to which I asked her if she meant about the hugs. She said yes, so I went on to explain my desire to give hugs to people and about my upcoming nine-day trip. She wished us good luck, and then off we went.

There weren't many pedestrians around, so after walking for a couple of blocks, we decided to go into the local Salvation Army Center, where there was a craft fair being held. Immediately, a woman holding a newborn baby approached us. Jace and I told her what we were doing, and she welcomed us and accepted hugs from each of us and then took pictures of us together. We walked through the craft fair and gave a few more hugs to vendors and customers. What a beautiful meeting, the Hugging Army and the Salvation Army!

After our time there, we continued walking through town. We were by the park in the center of town and noticed a large group of motorcycle riders heading to the Legion Hall directly across the street. I suggested that we cross the street and offer them hugs, which we did. About ten people, both men and women, accepted our offer and came over to receive hugs from either or both of us. We were even able to give a hug to a navy veteran who was in his wheelchair. Being able to, again, let go of a belief about who would hug us and who would not, and to experience that deep lesson with my son, was powerful and teeming with love.

That afternoon, I said a heartfelt goodbye to my son and headed off toward Asheville, North Carolina. I wanted to drive all the way to Asheville that day, but it was over five hundred miles, and I wasn't sure I would have the stamina for the entire journey. As it turned out, after several hours of driving, I stopped about two hundred miles short of Asheville to get some much-needed rest. I did *not* want to sleep! I was exhausted, but I didn't want to wind myself down and rest. I did sleep, and even though I was awake on and off throughout the night, I got seven hours of sleep.

10

Day 3: Asheville, NC (Part II) — 180 Miles

I woke up Sunday morning refreshed, excited, and ready to go! When I awoke, the world was topsy-turvy yet again. More bombings, more deaths, more feelings of fear and revenge in the atmosphere. I felt readier than ever to go to my beloved Asheville and to offer up what I felt inspired by. I began the last 180 miles of my journey.

What is it that calls to me most about the city of Asheville, North Carolina? First of all, it's the mountains. Her mountains. They're beautiful and mighty and hold secrets that only those tuned into Mother Nature herself can know. I have such honor and deep respect for those mountains. I have seen many mountains in my lifetime, on both the East Coast and West Coast, yet I have never seen anything like the Blue Ridge Mountains in my life. To see them as I drove down into the beautiful city of Asheville was such a welcome sight. I felt my inspiration come flooding in, along with deep emotion and gratitude. Asheville herself was only minutes away.

I had been to Asheville twice before, just in the previous three years, and I had loved it each time. As I drove along the highway, I found my way into downtown, as if it was in my very bones. I enjoy everything about this city—the music, diversity, culture, shops, and restaurants. I had decided that the first place I wanted to visit in the city was Pritchard Park, where Brenda and I had danced at a Friday-night drum circle the summer before. I parked in the same place as the previous summer and walked up to the park. It was under construction, so the sidewalks and other areas were surrounded by fencing and not very accessible. I stood in the middle of the seating area, holding my Free Hugs sign. There were not many people around that day, no tourists at all, and the people who were there appeared to have most of their belongings with them.

After a few moments, I decided to just walk around the city, wearing my sign. Within moments, a person who saw my sign asked me for a hug. At least every few minutes after that, as I walked around the city, people asked me for hugs. I also met some young people who wanted to have their pictures taken with me, as well as a group of friends who waved to me through a restaurant window to bring my hugs inside. I did just that. I gave out a few dozen hugs and business cards to several people that day, and I felt blissful yet not completely satisfied. In my two previous trips to Asheville, I had been there with my wife, Brenda. I missed her company. The sights just weren't as exciting without her to share it with in the moment. I drove to the area of the city called the River Arts District, which is old storefronts in the city that have been renovated and local artists have studios and workshops there. I gave one hug there, and as it started to rain, I decided to head in the direction of my next day's destination.

Day 4: Asheville, NC, to Greensboro, NC,
and onto Raleigh, NC—247 Miles

As I drove out of Asheville, I had mixed feelings about leaving, yet I believed that beginning the journey that night made sense. The rain continued and intensified as I drove toward Raleigh. At one point, it was sheets of water that were hitting my windshield, and I had to be very present, very alert, to continue in the storm. I had purchased a new CD from some local street musicians in Asheville, and I listened to that, which helped me focus. After I had fully listened to it, I drove along in the quiet, listening to the rain. One of the things that seemed quite profound for me on this trip was that my mind felt incredibly quiet. Usually, my mind is a constant swirl of thoughts, plans, ideas, and lists. Though there were times during my travels on the tour that I would project into the future or reflect on the past, I was able to come back to presence again and again.

11

The Conversation

I decided to stop in Greensboro, North Carolina, to spend the night and get a nice meal. I had hoped on my tour to stay with people, and when that didn't work out, I would stop when I was ready and get a hotel room for the night. It all fell into place precisely as it was intended. I found a hotel at a price that worked for my budget and decided to go find a place to have a nice meal and a glass of wine or two. I found the Olive Garden right down the street. I don't usually feel self-conscious eating by myself in a restaurant and decided to sit at the bar and enjoy the atmosphere there. I sat down and ordered a glass of Italian Chardonnay. I sipped it slowly, enjoying sitting and reflecting on the day and what was to come. As I sat there, I also documented my travels so far. I had committed to myself to write in my traveling journal each day, to keep close track of my adventures and the details that I knew I would want to remember someday.

As I waited for my meal, there were several customers that came in and out of the bar area, waiting for their food orders for takeout. One man in particular was standing, waiting for his order, right next to me. As he was waiting and enjoying a beer, he began talking with me about the woman he was in a relationship with and the challenges to relationships.

He seemed quite focused on the importance of relationships between men and women, and since that is not my relationship status, I just listened for quite some time. However, when he stated that he believed that all women need a man, I decided to speak up. I told him that I was married to a woman, and then he began to speak to me about the Old Testament of the Bible, and that the intention of God was for Adam and Eve to be together, man and woman, not Adam and Steve, man and man. I brought a conclusion to the conversation by stating that we simply had differing opinions, to which he asserted that his opinion was fact, and mine was not. To me, that was the end of it, with no drama or residue. I felt at ease in that moment about who I was, and there was nothing to defend or feel uncomfortable about. I went back to my writing and enjoying my dinner and wine. There was a woman sitting there, also having dinner, who left shortly before I did.

As I got ready to leave, I looked over to my right, and there was a handwritten note tucked under my purse. Although it seemed strange, I had the feeling that it was for me. I opened it up, and this is what it said:

Hello—

I couldn't help but overhear part of your conversation, and I just wanted to say that it was really wonderful hearing all the positive things you were saying as well as how patient and interested and open to discuss your life with the man beside you. I'm not sure I would be that patient or willing to listen to what he was saying. So thank you for what you were saying.

—Olivia (the person that was sitting beside you)

I was delighted that I was just doing what I do, and someone learned something from that and expressed their gratitude for it. A complete stranger to me. As I left the restaurant, the bartender thanked me and wished me luck on writing my book. I was floating out to my car, and as I drove out of the parking lot, I noticed a group of people standing together on the side of the building. I made eye contact with one of the men there, and as I did, he made an air gesture for a hug to me. I stopped the car, and many of the people in his group started laughing. I asked if he wanted a hug, and he did. Before I knew it, I was hugging each one of the people there—men, women, and children. They were shouting, cheering, and smiling as I walked up to them one at a time. I hugged a total of eight people, right there, in the span of about sixty seconds. It was incredible. I drove out of the parking lot, saying to myself, "I cannot believe my life!" I was allowing myself to experience the miracle of being completely open.

The next morning, I started out from Greensboro, toward my destination of Raleigh. I felt rested and completely at ease. I had slept really well, which is not typical for me when I travel, and even woke up early and went back to sleep. My schedule for the day was less pressing, as I had no scheduled gigs that day. After my shower, I got packed up and into my Hug Bug, then stopped across the street to get a coffee before getting on the road. After I got my coffee, I was walking back to my car, and a man was picking up garbage in the parking lot. He asked me if the car with the Free Hugs sign was mine, and when I said yes, he asked if there was a free hug available for him. I hugged him in the middle of the parking lot, and he wrapped his coat around me a bit, as it was cold. It was a beautiful moment with another human being and a great way to begin my day.

Because I didn't have far to travel to get to Raleigh, and I began early in the morning, I was ahead of my anticipated schedule. Spontaneously,

I decided to stop in the city of Durham, North Carolina, on my way. I found my way to Southpoint, which is a large, well-known mall in the city of Durham. I arrived before many of the storefronts were open. There were walkers in the mall, as well as employees arriving for work, and I was wearing my Free Hugs sign. I received a couple of hugs as I walked around inside. When I decided to head out to my car, there were some employees sitting outside of a restaurant, having a cigarette, and as I walked by, one of them called me back to get a hug.

I got to my car and continued my journey to Raleigh. I got some beeping horns, smiles, and waves on my last leg of the trip there. I had decided to begin my day in Moore Square Park, which is in an area of the city that is rich with restaurants and culture. I found it easily, and parking was available and free. Although it was a beautiful day, there were some rain clouds around, yet I was not worried at all. I knew that whatever happened, I would be cared for, and the experience would be amazing.

And so it was. I decided to stand in City Market, which was right near the park. I gave a couple of hugs and then decided to be adventurous and walk around that area of the city. I had two friends who lived near Raleigh, and they were going to join me for some hugging, so I spent some time exploring until they were due to arrive. What a great time I had! So many people walked by me, and it was around lunchtime, so there was a good amount of foot traffic. Some people made eye contact, some smiled, and some simply turned away and walked by. Others came right up to me with open arms, ready to give and receive a hug. I gave about ten hugs during that time and then decided to return to the park area to wait for my fellow huggers to arrive. It was a warm, humid day, so when the passing rainstorm came through, it felt refreshing!

My friends arrived a few minutes later, and after spending some time catching up with one another, we all decided to offer some hugs. I gave them each a Free Hugs sign, and we spread out a bit in the nearby area. There was a busy restaurant nearby and some people walking despite the raindrops. As my friends were getting comfortable with offering hugs, I wandered around town again. I had encouraged them to face their nervousness about doing hugs for the first time and to be as present as possible. By now, the lunch crowds were even more apparent. I walked by the courthouse, the capitol building, and several businesses and restaurants. I felt deeply at ease and in deep love and gratitude for having this experience. As I walked up and down the streets, I felt the light within me pouring out toward others around me.

Even when people did not approach me to receive a hug, I made eye contact with them and smiled. This was new for me, because I often felt like if someone did not want a hug, I would make them more uncomfortable by trying to catch their attention. Yet I wanted to connect with people, whether they were comfortable with hugs or not. And there were many people who were receptive to that. One young man saw me and said, "Free hugs?" I asked him if he would like a hug, and he broke out into the biggest, brightest smile, the best one I had seen so far that day. I kept feeling waves of love and connection between myself and other humans.

After going back to Moore Square Park and meeting up with my friends again, I decided I wanted to head to another place in the city called Pullen Park. I had family members who lived there years before, and it was one of my nephew's favorite places when he was a young child. It was close to where I was already in Raleigh, and I found it easily. As soon as I arrived there, it started raining hard. Again, with no immediate schedule that I was bound to, I just sat in my car and watched the deluge of rain hit my windshield. As I sat there, I gave my thanks to Mother Nature for always providing whatever it is that is needed. The rain kept falling, and the clouds were moving, and there was no doubt that the sun would eventually come out again, as always.

I am a big fan of carousels, and one of the reasons I found my way to Pullen Park was to ride the carousel while I was there. So, with the rain still falling, I got out of my car, bought myself a box of popcorn, and paid one dollar for a ticket to ride the carousel. There were not many people out that afternoon, and the park was quiet. Wearing my Free Hugs sign, I made my way to the carousel and gave a couple of hugs as I got ready to find my perfect horse. I always love riding the ones that move up and down and are on the outside, so I can see everything around me. The music was loud, and the lights were bright. Being in the moment and having an open heart and a quiet mind was a gift that I kept giving myself on the trip. Even though I had only just started a couple of days before, I had experienced so much beauty and connection already.

After Pullen Park, I headed to my friends' house for the evening. My fellow huggers from earlier that afternoon invited me to have dinner with them and to stay the night in their home. We had good food, listened to good music, played games, and got to enjoy each other. That night, I had another great sleep, so I was rested and ready for my next day of adventure!

12

Day 5: Raleigh, NC, to Charleston, SC—299 Miles

The next morning, after an evening of a lot of rain, it was beautiful. The sky was brightening up, and the air was cool and fresh. I was excited to begin the next part of my journey. I had never been to Charleston before, at least not that I remembered. I had always wanted to visit there, as its quaint, southern charm called to me. Moss-laden trees, historic homes, and southern hospitality all appealed to me. My mother was born and raised in the southern part of the United States, so I have always had an affection for it.

Being on the road for so many hours every day, I was never really sure how long a portion of the trip would take, due to traffic, stops, and weather. The trip from Raleigh to Charleston was a big longer than I expected, and although I didn't have anything formally scheduled until later that evening, I had wanted to go downtown to offer some free hugs. I tend to worry about having enough time a lot, and because my mind had been so quiet on this trip, I didn't want that to be a concern for me. I decided to just go ahead and head into the heart of the city. I wanted my first stop to be the Emanuel AME church in Charleston.

Almost two years before, a gunman entered the church during a prayer service on a Tuesday evening and shot several people, nine of which died from their injuries. The person who committed the act had stated he was attempting to start a race war. Where there had been so much hurt and loss, I believed it would be a good place to bring some healing hug energy.

When I arrived at the church, I was moved by how quaint and beautiful it was. I felt emotional and privileged to be there, knowing what they had endured. No one was at the church, and the area of the city where it was located was a busy main street, with very few pedestrians walking by. I took some pictures and waited for a reporter who wanted to come and do a story on my visit there but never showed up. I decided to leave and head to the heart of downtown to offer some free hugs.

It had been raining on and off all day, and when I found my

way downtown, it was still raining. The city seemed busy. I found parking and decided to walk around wearing my Free Hugs sign. It was lunchtime, and there seemed to be a lot of tourist activity. The streets and buildings appeared to be from a time long ago, and there were many shops, restaurants, and vendors around. I walked for a few blocks and found my way to an open-air marketplace where there were items of every kind for sale. I walked around, making my way through the crowds, and was asked for a couple of hugs.

As I headed out of town to my friend's house, to prepare for my evening program, I was aware of how sweaty and hot I was. My car had no air-conditioning, and the humidity was close to 100 percent. The colors from my skirt had actually run onto my white T-shirt. I was looking forward to getting a shower and getting ready for the evening. As I drove out of the city, I was trying to not be disappointed in how the day had turned out so far. Although I had released my expectations around my hugging experiences quite a bit, I still wished for things to be different than they were. I wanted dozens of people in the city of Charleston to have wanted a hug; I wanted there to have been congregants at the AME church to connect with and hug. As I breathed through my disappointment, I was also wanting there to be a good response for my evening program.

I have been friends with Julie, my host for the evening, for thirty years. She had grown up in Pennsylvania and moved to Charleston a few years before. It was great to see her and to be able to visit with her, even though it was for a short time. She was hopeful and excited about bringing my program to the church that she had been a member of since shortly after moving there. I got myself ready, we went and had some dinner, and then we drove over to the church. When we got there, the rain was relentless. There were no cars in the parking lot yet, so I unloaded the car and set up for my presentation. The pastor of the church came to introduce himself and greet us. I waited, excited to begin.

As it turned out, no one attended my presentation. The pastor and my friend Julie, who had never heard about my experience with the Hugging Army, listened as I told them the stories of my hugs and showed photos. I had hoped for a larger audience and yet was happy with how the evening unfolded, grateful for the lessons I was learning and how they were coming to me. The fact that I was eight hundred miles from home and talking about my hugging experiences was amazing to me. At the end of the evening, the pastor invited me to come back and be an active part of the Charleston Pride Festival. I returned to Julie's home that evening knowing that my travels were happening just as they were meant to and that whatever came next would be just as amazing.

13

Day 6: Charleston, SC, to Fort Payne, AL—413 Miles

I woke up the next morning, after having another good night's sleep and got myself ready for the next phase of my journey. I was driving to my furthest point south on this trip, the state of Alabama, where I had not visited since I was a teenager. As I drove there, I was deeply grateful for the life I was living. I felt so present in my experiences and what might happen next. Part of that gratitude and presence comes through the act of driving itself. I love to travel, and part of that love is driving; I enjoy it very much. Enjoying the scenery as I drive and having the freedom to go where I am called to is a blessing. As I drove along the highway, making my way south and west, I got a couple of thumbs-up from drivers as they passed me, and one air hug from a passenger in a car.

I have learned so much in my life through my experiences, and one of the deepest and most profound lessons for me is how to keep coming back to the present moment. It isn't just an idea; it is an actual way of being, action that I take so that I can remember to focus just on what is happening here and now. Growing up in the world, where I have learned to focus on the past or the future, that can be a real challenge for me. However, there is no peace within myself unless I remember that the present moment is all there ever is. My trip to Alabama was no exception; as I got closer to the city of Atlanta, Georgia, the traffic became denser, and although it's something I am used to from traveling so much, I started feeling scared. I felt scared that I would be late to my destination, and scared of getting in an accident. Yet, each time I remembered to just focus on the present moment and to be as alert and aware of my surroundings as possible, the fear would dissipate, and I found myself enjoying the journey once again. Gratitude is part of that process as well, when I remember that I have so many things to be grateful for, no matter what is going on around me—breath in my lungs, the ability to travel, and a deep love in my heart for who I am and what I am doing.

I had estimated it would be an eight-hour trip from South Carolina to Alabama, yet it was only seven hours, because when I crossed the Alabama border, I gained an hour due to being in the central time zone. Crossing that border felt so emotional to me, remembering that my mother and her mother were both born there. I stopped and took a photograph of my arrival there. I also realized as I drove into Fort Payne that I was driving along part of the Trail of Tears, hundreds of miles that Native Americans walked as they were forced from their lands to an area that the United States government had deemed was where they were to live. As I thought of all the souls that had traveled this land before me, I was again humbled and amazed at all the experiences I was having on this journey, ones that I could have never predicted.

Alabama is such a beautiful state. I drove through so many miles of mountains and deep, dark greens. I was amazed to see that armadillos are native in the wild there, and although I didn't see any alive, there were many of them dead on the side of the road. My friends who were hosting me that evening, Brandy and Kristy, were so welcoming and loving during my stay there. My hugging had brought me into their lives, and now I was speaking to their spiritual group about the Hugging Army.

The Wholistic Center, where I was speaking that evening, was a perfect place to bring my stories, pictures, and hugs. The remote property is dozens of acres, with lots of wooded areas. The founder of the center, Edwene Gaines, lived on the property. It was a working farm at one time, and then Edwene transformed it into a retreat center. In addition to the building where meetings, gatherings, and retreats were held, there was a small building on the property that served as a chapel; it had a beautiful stained glass window, statues, and candles, with plenty of seating inside. I saw images around the room of Christ, Buddha, and angels. It appeared as if all realms of spirit were welcomed there, which helped me to feel even more welcomed. There was also a large open field area where firewalks were held, led by Edwene.

The actual center, where I would be speaking, was open, spacious, and welcoming. There were persons already in the building, setting up for the potluck dinner. I was not sure that I would meet Edwene, but she was there, and it was a real thrill that she would be present for my discussion. I had read about her after being invited there, that she had struggled at times in her life and as a result had become a very giving, compassionate person. She loved to guide others in finding their own ways to abundance. In person, the love that radiated from her was astounding. She was shining.

As I set up, more and more people arrived. In total, about eighteen people were gathered for the evening. Many of those were members that attended regular meetings. It was nice to share a meal with all of them and have them each tell a bit about themselves as we had dinner. Some people were guests and first-time visitors like myself. One woman I met was visiting with her husband from Tennessee and told me that she had wanted to come because she had started an organization called Chattanooga Hugs to encourage connection with others, in person and virtually.

Shortly after dinner, I began my talk, "The Hugging Army: An Experience in Connection." I had brought a map that I created of all my destinations on this trip, and before it, I had my storyboards, photo albums, and copies of my news articles. As I started to talk about my experiences with hugs and show the photographs, it seemed like those listening were right there with me as I gave my first hug, blindfolded, to a small baby; as I talked about the young person who hugged me for a full minute; and as I shared the experience of hugging a homeless person who apologized for being stinky before I hugged her. There were nods of recognition in the audience, and they seemed to want to hear more. As I was talking, I felt tears in my eyes at times, remembering those deep experiences. I realized at that moment that I never had to worry again about "practicing" the stories prior to an event, that they flow from me when I trust deeply and allow myself to be vulnerable and in the present moment. I believe that vulnerability creates the power of my stories and experiences—the vulnerability of being seen and, therefore, truly seeing others as they are.

At the end of my talk, I played music on a CD that Brenda had recorded, which is her singing while playing her instrument, the harmonium. Although I had played other music in the past while my audience practiced mindful hugging, Brenda's music seemed to be the perfect pairing with the experience. I invited everyone to share present, mindful hugs with one another, and most of them decided to participate. A few of those hugs that evening brought flowing tears to my eyes, as I felt my heart crack open even more. Susan and Bill, the creators of Chattanooga Hugs, asked me to come and stay with them at their home in Chattanooga when they kicked off their first event for their organization. The center also asked me to come back again in 2018 to participate in a retreat and have the opportunity to be part of a firewalk. The evening had been magical in all respects. They even presented me with a love donation to assist with my travel expenses.

When we arrived back at my friends' home, I realized how tired I was from the day, yet it felt like I had done so much that the exhaustion was well worth it.

14

Day 7: Fort Payne, AL, to Charlotte, NC (or So I Thought)—290 Miles

I had another great night's sleep and woke up the next morning ready for the next phase of the journey. I was on my way by seven o'clock, central time, after waving goodbye to my new friends and hostesses. The plan was to drive through to Charlotte, North Carolina, my next destination. I expected to arrive there in the midafternoon and planned on going to a farmer's market in the city to give some hugs. Charlotte had been on my list from the first plans for the trip, and yet I was not feeling excited about or drawn to going there. When I crossed from Alabama into Tennessee, I stopped at a rest area to talk to Brenda and give myself some time and space to decide what I wanted to do.

Where I was in Tennessee was only 120 miles from Nashville. Of course, it meant going west, farther away from my next destination, yet I had never been there and was certain that visiting there would be unforgettable. I thought about it for more than a moment, what a spontaneous, fun detour it would be. After spending a few moments tuning in with myself more deeply, I realized that although I eventually wanted to visit Nashville and offer free hugs, I was being drawn toward continuing to drive east, heading toward Charlotte. At least that was what I thought. This day was one of my busiest on the road, with several car beeps, including from someone driving in a tractor trailer. I was feeling some excitement about my next experience with hugs, but it didn't feel like it was meant to be in Charlotte. There were no hints at feeling connected to going there, on this trip at least. I thought maybe it was because I was tired, but I wasn't sure, so I just kept on driving through the state of Tennessee.

Then I drove over the French Broad River. I thought immediately of Asheville. I thought of the beautiful mountains surrounding it. I thought of being in nature, more than in the middle of a city. When I crossed over the border into North Carolina, I stopped at the welcome center. I had been crying on and off for a few minutes because I was feeling pulled in by those mountains and Asheville herself. I sat down in the grass and finally realized that I was going to Asheville that day, not Charlotte. After all my planning and where it was I thought I was supposed to be that day, I had to follow my heart, my gut. Asheville was definitely where I needed to be and where I was being led to. I also decided that I would drive directly to the Biltmore Estate, wear my Free Hugs sign, and offer hugs there for the afternoon.

Before I left, I walked into the welcome center, and a young man pointed at me and told someone next to him I was the "hug lady," apparently from seeing my car. I went back and offered him a hug, which he gratefully accepted, as did the young woman with him. I told them a bit about my trip and my detour to Asheville, and they smiled as if they understood.

I drove directly to the Biltmore Estate, which is an eight-thousand-acre property in the heart of Asheville. Among gardens, paths, shops, properties, and the main house itself, there is a deep feeling of history, preservation, and nature. During my previous visit there, I had thoroughly enjoyed myself. I was surprised, and not surprised, that I was able to find my way there precisely, remembering it clearly from the previous summer's visit with Brenda. I drove up through the gates of the estate and went to the visitor's center to purchase my ticket. For a moment, I considered again if this was where I wanted to spend my afternoon; after all, it was a lot of money for admission to the estate, and I would only be there a few hours. However, I knew that I was supposed to be there. I just knew it in my heart.

I parked my car and walked up to the estate, with my sign on and an umbrella, as it looked like rain. I wanted to see the Biltmore Estate home, but my main destination was the gardens there. It started raining lightly, and as I was walking to the home, I noticed a tour group of students that were boarding their bus. As I walked across the lawn, two of the students approached me and asked if I was really giving free hugs, and if so, could they have one? I shared hugs with both of them. I knew yet again that I was precisely where I was supposed to be, receiving my first hugs in the first five minutes on the grounds. It just got better and better from there. When I first entered the home, a young woman commented on my sign and received a hug when I offered it to her.

I walked through the entire estate home with my sign on. There was a good crowd of people there that day, and when I came out of the home, there was another group of touring students, and they all came over to get a hug. Then I walked to the gift shops and the restaurants, and when I encountered some more students from the group, they came up to me, one after another, wanting a hug! It was amazing, and the entire group even posed for a picture with me. Shortly after our photo, one of the chaperones asked me, "Are you a Christian?" I responded, "I believe in Jesus. I actually believe in a lot of things." She then said something to me about spreading love and how that's all that really matters. In the past, I often got uncomfortable when a person I encountered related being a good person with being Christian or some other religious affiliation. Now, the more secure I was standing in being just who I am, the less it mattered and the more I could let the other person be precisely who they are as well.

As I walked across the grounds, the rain continued lightly, and I headed for the gardens, with one person asking for a hug along the way.

I had only been to the Biltmore Estate once before, and the gardens had been breathtaking at that last visit. This time, many of the plants and flowers were just beginning to fill in, but the roses were varied and abundant. The smells and sights of these lovely flowers were so inspiring to me. There are also arbors in the center of the gardens, and I sat under there for a while, closed my eyes, and listened to the birds nearby. A family of three came by, and the man asked me about the hugs and why I was giving them. All three of them accepted a hug from me.

Down below the gardens, there is a stream that runs through the woods, and I walked down there. Brenda and I had discovered it the summer before during our visit and sat by it for a while. The path was wet and quiet, and I was getting my full dose of nature that I deeply needed. I listened to the running water, and a cardinal came by, sat on the branch of a tree nearby, and chirped to me for a couple of minutes. I felt like he was a reminder to keep focusing on my dreams and to remain inspired. As I walked back to the car, a few more students came by for another hug as they were going to their buses to leave. What a magical time.

As I was getting ready to leave the estate, I wanted to stop at another area called Antler Village. There are several shops there, as well as restaurants and a winery. I wasn't sure yet where I was staying for the night and had time to stroll and see the sights. As I walked through the village, a woman approached me for a hug. I browsed for a few minutes and decided to leave the estate and go into downtown Asheville. As I walked back to my car, I gave a few more hugs and even was asked to pose for a picture with a couple of people. They asked me about what I was doing, so I told them about my trip and answered some questions about my inspiration for doing it. In every simple interaction with other people, I was reminded of how grateful I was to be doing what I was doing in that moment.

I found my way to downtown Asheville easily, parked the car, and put on my sign. My immediate goals were dinner, wine, and to make my plan of where I was sleeping for the night. I really wanted to either camp for the evening or stay in a hostel, which I had never done before. The sky had cleared nicely, and the air was fresh and cool. I found a great restaurant in town and got to sit outside. The meal was delicious, including home-cooked biscuits and blueberry jam. After my meal, I walked around town and found my way to the hostel that was right around the corner. I rang the doorbell and waited, but no one answered or came to the door. I was a bit nervous thinking about staying there, so I accepted this as a sign that I was meant to stay somewhere else. I decided I would either find a campground near town or start driving toward Greensboro and look for a hotel.

Again, the rains came as I drove out of town. It was pouring rain as I left the city. I realized that a campground would not be an option in that weather! There were some familiar exits as I drove toward Greensboro, which was only two hours away. On the highway, the driver of a tractor trailer gave me a beep. I felt relaxed and at ease about whatever was going to come my way next.

I decided to stop near Marion, North Carolina, and pulled off at the exit. As I did so, a car behind me started flashing its lights, I presumed at me. When I was stopped at the end of the exit ramp, the driver pulled up beside me. The passenger-side window went down, and the passenger asked, "Can I get a hug?" When I said yes, the young man said, "Seriously?" He got out of his car, and we hugged right there in the middle of the exit ramp. He smiled and said, "Bless you," and we were both on our way. It was a beautiful ending to a lovely day. I found a clean, comfortable hotel and was able to write out my postcards and make some plans for the next couple of days of my trip.

During my travels, my trust in myself deepened. I understood more deeply that when I listen, *really listen*, to what it is that feels right to me, on a level that is deeper than my intellect, I am always led to what is the right path, to where I need to be, and to where it feels most right. That is not easy to put into words, because it is something that happens to me that is beyond words. Some may call it faith or a higher power. All I know is that it never fails me when I really trust that inner voice.

15

Day 8: Asheville, NC, to Greensboro, NC—172 Miles (2,143 Total Miles So Far!)

When I considered how many miles I had traveled on the tour, I was amazed and excited to think about how far I had gone, all the adventures I had had, and all the people I had met in just eight short days. I was ready for travel, despite not sleeping well the night before; I had been up late and was up early. The surroundings of my hotel were so beautiful—deep, lush greens everywhere. I had some breakfast and sent off two-dozen postcards to friends and family, and then I was on my way. From Marion, North Carolina, to Greensboro was a short trip, and as I got closer to the exit for the downtown area, I started to feel scared. I was nervous that I would get lost. Of course, I did not get lost. I found my way to the downtown area, right near the civil rights museum. The street that I parked on, South Elm Street, was sweet and historic. There was beautiful mural art on the wall of the building right near where I parked, depicting music and culture from the local area.

And just like that, I felt scared again. As I was getting out of my car, I felt a sense of nervousness. Would I be judged for walking around the city with my Free Hugs sign on? Of course, it is always possible that others don't understand what I am doing and may even hold a judgment about it. Yet I believed in what I was doing. So, I paused, took a deep breath, and reminded myself of my true intention: to connect with others. I put my sign on and started walking.

Within minutes, a person approached me on the street for a hug. And that was just the beginning. I received quite a few hugs while I was there in Greensboro, one of the cities on the tour where I had never been before. As I walked around, a fire truck went by, and as it passed, one of the firemen waved to me. As I kept walking, they had parked the truck and gotten out to have lunch at a local restaurant. The fireman who had waved to me came up to me on the sidewalk and said, "I need a hug today." I said, "That's why I'm here." I hugged two other fire personnel as well. It was beautiful and connected. The people of Greensboro were so friendly and abundant. Easy smiles were the norm, in a way that stood out on the trip so far.

I also decided, while I was there, to visit the International Civil Rights Museum. It is housed in the former Woolworths department store, and the museum was actually built around the lunch counter in the store that was the scene of many civil rights sit-ins back in 1960. I learned so many new things about the history of the civil rights movement, local to there, and I also felt inspired by the courage and resilience of many of the people involved. As I left the museum, I hugged a couple more people. Then I went down the street and had a robust cup of coffee at a local shop called Green Bean.

As I finished up my time there, I decided that I would start driving toward Hurdle Mills, which was my next destination. I was excited to find a campground for the night, to sleep under the stars and the full moon and even build a fire. On the highway, I received many beeps, smiles, and waves as people drove by, and I even got a hug from a person at a rest area. I was fully expecting to find a campground nearby, but there were none off any of the exits of the interstate, nor any in the immediate area of Hurdle Mills. I had chosen that as my next destination because there was to be a lavender festival at a local farm the next day. I had never been to one and thought it would be an amazing place to offer free hugs. I had no success even finding where the farm was located and decided to revise my plan a bit.

I was in the vicinity of Durham, North Carolina, and decided I would find a grocery store, buy something for dinner, and have a picnic at a local park to get my fill of nature that I was craving. Yet I started feeling fear again, about the local area that I was driving through and about the drivers all around me as I tried to find my way. I decided to just get back on the interstate, start driving, and see where I felt inspired to land. I found my way to Chapel Hill, North Carolina, another city I had never visited. I stopped at a restaurant and got a feast of salad, avocado, hummus, tortilla chips, salsa, and white wine. I also found a hotel right nearby that was easily in my price range. As I fed myself and rested for the evening, I caught up with some friends on Facebook about my most recent adventures. Again, by being present to what I was feeling in the moment and trusting my instincts, I landed right where I was meant to be for the night.

16

Day 9: Greensboro, NC, to Hurdle Mills, NC, Durham, NC, and Chapel Hill, NC (Detour)—One Hundred Miles

Beautiful sleep. That is what I had that night. Knowing that I had listened deeply to my inner voice and landed in just the right place for the day brought a deep sense of peace to me, allowing me to get the rest I really needed. As I was getting ready to begin my adventure to the lavender festival, hoping to meet up with a new friend of mine that lived nearby in Raleigh, I discovered that admission to the lavender festival was by reservation only, and I had not made one. They were already booked for that day. The day was gorgeous, warm, and inviting, so I decided—again, by deeply listening to that still, present voice within—that I would visit downtown Chapel Hill and offer hugs there. Then I would travel to Raleigh and have lunch with my friend Lauren. By allowing things to unfold, rather than trying to plan every step, I allow the miracle to emerge. I got ready as I listened to birds singing outside of my hotel window.

Before I went to town, I stopped at the local CVS to pick up a couple of things. I asked the cashier the way to downtown and told her why I was there. She accepted a hug from me, and I left her my card so she could keep following me. I then found my way to the center of Chapel Hill, which is a large college community, though that day was relatively quiet. There were many storefronts, restaurants, and cafes, and there were many people out and walking around town. I received around fifteen hugs while in Chapel Hill, my first one from a man who hugged me as we were both in the crosswalk of a busy street. Again, it had been the perfect stop for this day's journey.

I started back on the road and headed toward Raleigh. I was meeting my friend at an outdoor mall, at a special restaurant she wanted me to try with her. While I was waiting for her, I walked around, wearing my Free Hugs sign, and got some beautiful smiles and positive comments from people. Lauren and I had never met in person and had been introduced through social media by a mutual friend. Over the year or so that I had followed her, I came to understand that we were kindred spirits. That became even more apparent when we met in person. We talked for hours, about all types of subjects. We understood our connection once we got to spend some one-on-one time together. We took pictures and shared dessert.

As we were getting ready to part and I was bracing for my four-hour drive to Virginia, a young woman came up to me and said, "I apologize for interrupting, but I think I saw you at the Biltmore." I asked her if we had hugged there, and she said yes! She proceeded to show me a picture on her cell phone, the group photo we had taken before I left the estate that day. It was one of the most sweet, amazing moments of my trip, to see her twice, in places hundreds of miles from each other! I asked if I could hug her again and then asked her parents, who were with her, if it was okay for her to share the picture with me, to which they said yes.

Lunch in Raleigh had not even been on my schedule. I expected to be smelling lavender all afternoon and hugging people in rural North Carolina. I had just finished telling Lauren that there had been so many amazing moments on the trip so far, most of which I could have never planned and that were above and beyond my itinerary. That is when Sophia, the young woman who approached me, came to the table. It was nothing less than pure magic.

After we said our goodbyes, I began my journey toward Vienna, Virginia, which is where I would be staying that evening. It was just a few miles north and east of Washington, DC, and a great place to rest for the night before the last day of my tour. The ride to Vienna was long, and the weather was hot. Yet the ride was peaceful and uneventful, and I arrived safely at the hotel I had chosen for the evening. I brought my bags into the hotel and was checking in when a man at the front desk engaged me in conversation. He noticed a button that I had on my purse; it was the logo for Chattanooga Hugs, the organization that my friend Susan had started there. He asked me about what it was and then proceeded to ask me about my T-shirt. At the time, I was wearing one of my Hugging Army T-shirts, with the logo, and with Free Hugs printed on the back. I told him about the Hugging Army, about my Hug Bug tour, and where I had been so far. I also gave him my business card, and he asked me if I had given many hugs so far. I told him I estimated that I had given and received 350 hugs so far on the trip. He then told me, "It's about to be 351. I could really use a hug." So I hugged him there in the lobby. It was another beautiful moment, in the moment. I again felt a deep sense of gratitude for all the experiences that I was allowing myself on this journey of my life. I settled into my room, got comfortable, and had a great few hours of sleep.

17

Day 10: Raleigh, NC, to Vienna, VA, then Washington, DC—280 Miles

In the morning, I was up early, excited for the events of the day. I was both exhausted and energized. Today felt like one of the most exciting for me; I was going to spend hours with thousands of other people, walking in pride and solidarity in DC, and then I would be driving home to see my beloved wife after ten days of being apart. After showering, having some breakfast, and packing up my car for the final time this trip, I started driving to the train station. I was meeting a friend from Scranton who was coming to Washington for the National Pride March that day. She and some friends were driving down that morning, and we were all going to ride the train together into the city. I had done my homework, finding where it was easiest to get into Washington by train, fairly close to the march location, and still allowing the ability to get out of the city easily as well. I had also researched which train we would be riding, although since I don't travel by train that often, I had some anxiety about getting on the wrong one. I reminded myself, yet again, that coming back to the present moment is always my saving grace, no matter what is gripping me at the time.

Kelsey and her friends arrived early that morning, having departed from home at four o'clock. We all parked near the train station and headed over to where we would be departing from. The air was already incredibly warm, and it was to be a sunny, hot day in the city. My friend had never ridden on a train before. I had taken both subways and above-ground trains and always had an enjoyable time, riding along and wondering about other people and where they were going. I presumed that others on the train with us that morning were also going into the city; many of them were carrying rainbow pride flags and wearing various T-shirts depicting something about lesbian, gay, bisexual, and transgender identities. I had been to several pride events before, yet I felt the excitement of being with so many other people in visible signs of solidarity and love.

As we got off the train at the stop that I had hoped would put us near the march, I was pleasantly surprised to see that we were literally at the place where it was starting. We arrived with plenty of time to find a place to walk from and to look around and take in the sights. There was a diverse collection of people there that day, and everyone was carrying some symbol of LGBT support and pride. The energy in the street felt like electricity; it was palpable.

The sun was already fully upon us, and it was hot at ten in the morning. As the march was getting ready to start, many people began cheering and shouting. As I looked up, the vision of equality and rainbow flags against a cloudless blue sky was breathtaking. We started to move as a group, but it was slow going, as so many people were in the streets. The breadth of the march was fifteen to twenty people across, and in length, it seemed to take up a few city blocks. As a united group, we walked, we shouted, and we waved our banners. People were holding hands and holding signs. There were also many people along the route who were standing on the sidewalks, simply watching people walk by. Some were waving and clapping in support. There were so many smiling faces that day!

I gave a couple of hugs to people as we walked along through the city. Yet I was feeling inspired to be more available for hugs, instead of walking and offering them. As my companions stopped to look for souvenirs, I stood on the side of the city street, arms open, offering hugs to others. It did not take long for people who were walking along the march route to approach me and get hugs. I was standing there for around twenty minutes, and as the marchers passed by, dozens of them stopped for a hug. Many of them were in costumes or with groups of their friends. Many smiled as they approached me, appearing open and ready, and some even whispered to me, "Bless you," "Thank you," and "I love you." My heart was overflowing right then, not only through the offering of hugs to other people but also from what I was receiving each time someone hugged me or simply smiled at me and waved as they walked by. More than once, I felt tears of gratitude and joy well up in my eyes. A person hugging me held on just a bit longer than the rest, and I actually felt our hearts beating, almost in unison. The magic of the moment was again visiting me, simply because I was allowing it to enter.

I found myself being curious throughout the day about what leads a person to enter into my outstretched arms for a hug, and others to walk by. I knew for certain that I had let go of my beliefs that certain groups of people will or won't be willing to hug me. I firmly believe that, as human beings, we all need and desire not only hugs but frequent, loving physical contact. However, I also know that for many people, that type of contact stirs up feelings of fear, so they cannot connect even with themselves and their feelings or desires, let alone physically connect with another person, particularly one who is a stranger to them.

And I can more than identify with feelings of fear. I can identify with that craving to be vulnerable and yet the fear that my vulnerability leaves me exposed and in danger. I had felt fear many times on the trip. That day, I felt a sense of fear as I walked with thousands of other people past the White House and saw that there were Secret Service agents on the roof, holding either cameras or guns. I could not tell for sure. I also believed that a city this large, with this visible of an event going on, could be a prime target for some type of physical violence. Yet I never saw one protestor or one threat of physical violence over the several hours. I knew that this city and this event were the perfect final stop on the Hug Bug tour.

As my friends and I continued to walk along the marching route, I stopped every few minutes, facing the oncoming masses, and held my arms out, with my Free Hugs sign showing on my chest. That simple gesture was an invitation to love, to presence, to peace, and for some, to refuge. At one point in the day, I was standing on the side of the street, and an LGBT marching band from New York walked by. I had to step back, there were so many of them. Two persons that were with the band slowed down to hug me, and one put an acrylic, amber-colored heart into my hand.

We continued to follow the marching route, which walked us through various areas of the city and landed in front of the Capitol and the Washington Monument. We posed for pictures, along with all the other tourists who seemed to be in the city that day. We found our way to the rally, where there were speakers and many marchers sitting under the trees that were on either side of the Mall. It was a hot summer day and a great place to seek some shaded area. In that moment, I felt so present and so alive. Instead of feeling frustration at the belief that the world at large did not understand who I was, I felt compassion for anyone who believed the world didn't see them at all. I was not identifying with myself as a lesbian marching among my gay, straight, and transgender brothers and sisters, but as a human being loving my fellow humans. It felt like barriers of all kinds, within myself and those around me, kept being broken down and left behind.

It had been such a full, hot, and amazing day. As my friends and

I got on an outbound train, headed back to Virginia to make our way home, we felt filled with emotion, excitement, and connection. As I got back in my Hug Bug for the last time this trip, I thought about the trip in its entirety and all the gifts that had come to me as a result of being open and available. It was as if a deep, soulful part of me was waiting to be more fully discovered, and it had certainly opened up more on this ten-day tour. I had learned to listen more deeply to that inner self, and I would never again be able to ignore its calling. I was so tired yet so grateful to be driving north and east, toward my home, toward my family, and toward the first chapter of putting my new lessons to the test.

18

The Lessons

Several weeks after returning home from my Hug Bug tour, I was able to put to paper what some of my deepest lessons had been from the trip, and all the experiences within it.

Lesson 1: Being in the present moment is of the utmost importance.

One of the biggest lessons for me on this journey was the importance of being in the present moment. I have been learning and studying about present-moment awareness more deeply in the last few years of my life, and the trip allowed me to put it into practice more consistently and deeply. During my travels, I had long periods of time in the car, with no companion along for the ride. I would turn off my music or my talking books and just be in the silence of the moment. During those times of silence, I had thoughts about where I was going to next, what I had done the day before, or about being tired, hungry, or both. But often, I just drove along, aware of the experience in the moment. Visually, the trip was so beautiful, and I was able to allow myself to enjoy that by being as present in the moment as possible. Also, the more present I was, the more I was able to enjoy and notice when someone in a passing car would wave, honk their horn in support, or even offer me a hug through their window. Being present allows me to really see, hear, and experience the world as it is. When I see, hear, and experience the world as it is, I am less judgmental of those around me.

When I noticed myself not being in the present moment, I almost always found that the feeling of fear was present. Fear does nothing but get in the way of deeply loving and accepting myself and where I am at, and as a result, loving and accepting those around me. The fears I experienced most often were fear of rejection, fear of retaliation, fear of being alone, fear of not being enough. What I know about fear is that, ultimately, every fear is a fear of death, whether it is fear of physical death, the death of an idea, or the death of a way of being.

Presence has become more than just a concept to embrace when I remember to do so; it has become essential for my inner peace. When I am not being in the present moment fully, I am instead deeply immersed in telling some type of story to others, about something that is of utmost importance to me. Or I am projecting into the future about what might happen, or I am focusing and dwelling on past events in my life. The past and the future, and my thoughts about either or both of them, will never serve me properly to enjoy my life. What works for me is remaining in the here and now, as often as I am able to remember to do so. And yet everything around me tries to grab my attention to pull me out of the present moment. Our egos do not want us to be in the present moment, because doing so means letting go of all the stories we have built up that describe our identity or who we believe we are. Present-moment awareness threatens the ego because it reminds us that we are not the identity we have built ourselves up to be.

When I stand in a space with my arms wide open, or when I walk down a city street with my Free Hugs sign around my neck, and I am fully in the present moment, it doesn't matter if anyone hugs me or not.

In my gesture of love and openness, I am being my truest self in the world.

Lesson 2: Whatever emotion I am experiencing at any given time, I can feel it completely, and nothing bad will occur because of that.

Another lesson that I learned more deeply on this journey was that whatever emotion I am experiencing at any given time, I can feel it completely, and nothing bad will occur because of that. I had moments during the trip when I felt afraid, uncertain, or self-conscious and insecure. Although those emotions felt uncomfortable, I stayed with them until they subsided. What I understand more fully is that when I experience any emotion at all, it is a temporary state of being, which means it will eventually go away. It means I don't have to be afraid to have feelings of sadness, despair, or uncertainty.

Any feeling that does not feel like peace or contentment is connected to some sort of fear within. When I am able to recognize that fear for what it is, I can fully surrender and then accept it, and it dissipates quickly. When I resist the feeling or attempt to figure it out, it seems to take longer for it to resolve. Although I feel fear less often in my life, I know that I will, most likely, never be fully free of fear. However, I can know that it will eventually cease and that I can go on even if I am scared. When I let my fears be in charge, I often create additional emotions or scenarios in my mind, which I focus on more than the passing of the emotion and what is happening right now. When I fully feel my emotions, meet and love myself right where I am, and remember that my experience is unique to me and has nothing to do with anyone else, I am truly free. I am free to be who I am, in the moment, without blame, judgment, or resentment, and with the trust and the knowing that any state is temporary in nature.

Lesson 3: Vulnerability is the only way to deep, pure love.

Vulnerability is the only way to deep, pure love. I learned this even more deeply on my trip and have continued to learn it each day since my return from the trip. When I open up my heart fully and willingly by being myself and being open with that, love pours both out of and into me. While I was traveling, I had countless open, vulnerable moments, many of which I have written about here.

When I use the word *vulnerable*, I mean a few different things. I know that I am being most vulnerable when I am purely myself in the company of others, no matter if the person is a friend or a stranger to me. When I remember that there is no need for me to hide aspects of who I am, that is vulnerability to me.

To have a conversation with a person whose views about love and relationships are significantly different from my own, and to hold my own space gently and powerfully, that is vulnerability to me.

To stand in front an audience of two people and speak about my experiences with hugging, when I had desired and anticipated a larger crowd, that is vulnerability to me.

When I am driving to a destination that I don't feel connected to, and I leave the planned path for a deeper calling, that is vulnerability.

And when I stand on a street, or in a room, with my arms open and my Free Hugs sign on my chest, or I just walk down the street with it on, that is pure vulnerability. My willingness to shine my love from within allows miracles to enter. So many beautiful circumstances continue to unfold in my life the more often I remember this essential state of being.

I am definitely aware of the moments when I don't want to be vulnerable, because in that moment, I am afraid of that level of presence, and I fear leaving behind my beliefs of how I thought I had to be in the world in order to be "safe." In that form, I have enjoyed the familiarity, the feeling of protection, and the ability to control. When I invite presence and vulnerability in, however, there is no need for protection and no need to know what will happen next. I don't have to control anything, and I can release my expectations. I can allow myself to be as I am, and therefore others to be as they are.

Recently, I began to offer hugs at a local hospital, in the intensive care unit waiting area. When I stood there for the first time, with my Free Hugs sign around my neck and my arms open and available, I felt self-conscious. I also felt a sense of not being sensitive to the needs of those who were waiting, believing that my offering might be viewed as whimsical or uncaring. However, doctors and family members alike have come to me for hugs. Some people have cried or prayed in my arms. When I let go of judgment, expectation, and control, and stay completely present and open, miracles have the space to fly in.

Lesson 4: It's best not to get attached to a preferred or predicted outcome of a situation.

I have also learned more deeply about not getting attached to a preferred or predicted outcome of a situation. When I first began planning for the Hug Bug tour, I was doing it in response to how people had received the Hugging Army and my experience at my first-ever Fringe Festival in Scranton. After the festival, I had more expansive ideas about what connection means to me, and I was very excited at the thought of sharing that with other people across the country. As I shared earlier in the book, my initial idea was that I would travel to parts of the East Coast where various friends of mine live, and I would work with my friends to secure venues where I could talk about the Hugging Army with groups of people. I also thought I would charge a fee at the venues, in order to help with my travel expenses. However, when I wasn't coming from a place of fear about money, the bigger part of me was sure that my offering should be free of charge. With that in mind, I just started reaching out to friends in various places and let them know what I would need: just a space and an electric source.

As venues were not coming together, and as the worry and discouragement grew in me about how I had wanted the tour to turn out, I knew that I had to choose another perspective. I wanted to enjoy this trip, no matter what. And if my enjoyment of it was dependent on how I wanted it to be, I was sure to be disappointed.

Finally, I let go of my desired outcome. I decided to completely surrender what it was I hoped and wanted to happen. I made a clear decision about when I would leave and where I would go, regardless of whether or not I had a scheduled venue. I would explore, participate in adventure, and be as spontaneous as possible.

Being spontaneous about such a passionate project was a new concept for me. I often thought of myself as the queen of control. I like order, organization, and scheduling. I enjoy planning for something and will get lost in the details of it. Actually, what I love about it is the belief that I have power over the future. I understand that any belief suggesting I can know what the future holds is an illusion. Letting go of the outcome, or the preferred outcome, not only brings me peace; it is the only truth. The truth is that nothing exists outside of this moment, right here and right now. When I forget this truth, either unconsciously or out of fear of feeling powerless, I have no peace. I simply have a belief that everything around me is at my command.

I also came to understand that the more that I am anticipating or hoping for a specific outcome to occur, in order to be happy with it, the more that I am stifling the magic that is bound to unfold spontaneously. I have been amazed and awestruck each time I have remembered to let go of the outcome and to just be as present as possible. Magic happens in places I would least expect it. I understand now that I have been taught that I have control over things outside of myself, and now that I know that it is not true, I can have deeper compassion for those who still hold that to be true. I have so much gratitude for learning to let go. In the act of letting go of circumstances around me, I have experienced a love of self and an inner peace like I have never known. It is a true miracle and will continue to carry and sustain me through anything that is not yet known to me.

Being attached to any outcome is a manifestation of fear of the unknown and a denial of the impermanence of life. It is also denial of the present moment being the only thing that ever is. When I think about something in the future, I get scared. If it is something that I am looking forward to, it is fear that it will not turn out the way that I desire. These fears wake me up in the night, and sleep only returns to me when I remember the truth that this moment, right now, is all there ever is.

The reflection on the past also comes from fear, because I am either grieving something that has passed away or am longing for something in the present or in the future that is similar to or the same as the past. I get afraid of things changing, which of course they always do. And I get afraid that what I have now won't be the same as what it was in the past. Therein also lies the beauty of life. Impermanence. Change. The unknown. This means to me that anything, at any time, is possible. Endless options of what could possibly come next in my life are at the ready. Yet, at the same time, I only need to choose the best step I need to make right now. I don't need to choose in this moment by keeping tomorrow or next week in mind. I just have to be in this moment; that is all that is needed. That is always enough; actually, it is always more than enough.

Lesson 5: I have come to an understanding of my sameness with other human beings.

Another lesson that has come my way, through my experiences of hugging people over the last couple of years and through the Hug Bug tour, is the understanding of my sameness with other human beings. For much of my life, I saw myself as different from those around me. At times, that difference felt like me being odd in comparison to others, in relation to how I acted or dressed, or what I believed. I also felt a sense of difference, compared to others, in the way that I related to people who appeared to have some obvious struggles in life. As a social worker by education and profession, I was taught, and came to believe, that there were always persons who were less fortunate than I was. And in addition to that difference between us, there was also the difference that I had the capacity to help them, because they could not help themselves. This set up some destructive presumptions in my mind over the years. I believed, for a very long time, that other human beings were not capable of caring for or helping themselves. I also created a false belief about myself, which was that I was the hero who would lead people in need to the light. I saw myself as better, or at least more capable, than they were. Even though I saw this as a way to be loving and caring toward people in need, I was actually seeing myself as different, better, or in a higher position of sorts.

When I first began offering hugs to others, here in the city in which I live, I still saw myself as different, as unique and special. I liked that I felt special, and I believed that my offering of hugs was a gift to them, one they were not able to give to themselves. I wanted to save the world from itself, in a way, and to bring to it comfort and peace. I had built a solid identity around what I called the helper, the giver, and the healer. Having those identities allowed me to see people who needed me as helpless. In reality, many people do feel helpless, because they have learned and believed that they needed someone else, in this case me, to heal them from whatever was hurting them. It was as if both of us, the other person and I, were invested in maintaining the bond between us in that way. I was certainly invested in it, as I saw it as who I was. It was my career and what I had studied in college at both an undergraduate and graduate level. I also saw it as who I was in my personal and family relationships as well.

To alternately see my sameness with every single person around me has been a beautiful blessing in my life. It has enabled me to connect with other people in a deeper, more authentic way. When I am truly myself with others, be they strangers, friends, or clients, it creates an immediate heart connection between us. When I embrace another human being, purely in a gesture of love and connection, I realize that I am never alone. I feel a mutual understanding of oneness, which lies deeply beneath all our physical forms and personal identities. In that instant, I feel our sameness.

I used to intellectualize my sameness with another person as a concept, not ever really feeling it or believing it. I kept my distance from it, getting lost in the physical form of myself and others, and using that to see myself and others as clearly separate beings. When I hug, I experience the feeling of sameness like I never have before. In that moment, I don't need to solve any problem or fix anything that to me seems broken. Actually, in that moment, everything is whole, and there is no illusion of brokenness or need. What is available from each of us is offered, and what is needed is taken. And the exchange and sharing is happening for those few seconds of a physical embrace. It is wondrous to experience and to behold.

Of all the lessons I have learned through hugging, and more deeply while on the Hug Bug tour, is to love my self, precisely as I am. I have read books, written affirmations, studied to be a life coach, gone to events, and talked to others about how we "learn" to love ourselves. I believe the truth is we don't have to learn anything about that. We already know how to love ourselves, but we forget how to do that over years of "education" and accepting outside knowledge as the truth about who we are.

I can remember being a child. One of the things that I remember, not in my intellectual memory but in my pure essence, is that I was happy. I felt love and that I was loved. I felt connected to others. I felt grief and confusion, presence and joy and curiosity. The details of what I did as a child are hazy to me, and memory is never fully accurate anyway. But I do remember how it felt to be me, from a very early age.

Slowly but surely and methodically, I was carefully taught, by family, friends, church, and school. I was taught exactly what my teachers in life learned, as they were taught based on what their teachers of life had learned. Among those teachings were learning the difference between what is "right" and what is "wrong." Many of them were taught, as I was, that the only way to stay safe and healthy is to live in a state of fear, alertness, and vigilance. We all were taught that some people matter more than others. That family is everything and will always be there for you.

Sometimes I believe that the bigger error is not that we teach what we believe but rather the *certainty* of that belief—the belief that no other possibilities exist. In theory, I guess it makes sense that we as human beings attach ourselves to certain beliefs and identities. Those beliefs and identities have helped me to feel safer and more connected in my lifetime, and my beliefs have confirmed for me when I meet other people who think, act, feel, look, and believe as I do. There have been many times when my feeling of belonging with others actually became an identity for me, to be part of a group where I felt understood and appreciated.

More recently, however, I have embraced my uniqueness, my sense of being odd and different. This was enhanced during the Hug Bug tour when I felt fearful or discouraged and believed that others needed to embrace me, literally and figuratively, for me to feel loved and purposeful. However, when I moved beyond my fears, I found that I loved myself more deeply, precisely as I am, in all my uniqueness and various forms. This lesson also serves as a reminder that I can only ever love myself; to hold others accountable to love me in a certain way, with conditions or expectations, is a setup for them and for myself. In addition to that, I can never love or accept others as they are until I love myself just as I am, in a deep and true way.

However, the lesson of loving myself is not the end of the story. I need to keep remembering that in that love, if I see myself as unique or odd, I am focusing on the form, the identity, and therefore strengthening my belief in being separate from others. Inherent in my love of self must be my understanding and acceptance of my universality, the knowing that all of us are one. We are from the same source, the same energy, the same entity. In loving myself in an authentic way, I see my true essence, the essence that I share with every other living being, and I stop seeing myself as a separate human form, alone.

When I offer hugs to others and talk about the importance of hugs and the power of human connection, I talk about how hugs relate to oneness. When I hug another person, friend or stranger, I remember, recognize, and understand that we are not separate beings. In our physical forms and in the structure of our lives and personalities, we are separate. However, when two people join together in a connection, we see and experience the feeling of sameness. Hugs are a deep reminder to me that I am not separate from others, they are not separate from me, and I am never alone.

I believe that my lessons learned from the Hug Bug tour will continue to unfold and be realized. Being on the road alone for ten days opened me up to so much possibility of learning and awareness. I learned then, and continue to learn, how important it is for me to be inspired and to go where it is that I am led. I used to crave structure and routine. I was never comfortable with being spontaneous. And even though I was aware of my gut feelings and instincts, I rarely followed them. I would follow an instinct, or what I thought was that, only when it came as an impulse to create something new in my life. It didn't feel relaxed as much as a reaction to what I thought I should do next, to not miss an opportunity or out of fear or panic. I did this in terms of relationships, jobs, and moving from one place to another. The results and lessons were always rich and meaningful, especially when it did not turn out as planned or as I had hoped. That was often the case.

However, being inspired, or going where I am led, is not an intellectual experience. It is not something that I think about doing, and it does not come from a space of fear, lack, or reaction. For me, it is becoming still and present. It is deeply listening to what I want on a feeling level, one that is difficult to put into words. It is not always logical, and it is most often not part of any plan that I or other people have had for me. When I am doing that which inspires me, I am connected to my passion for life. I feel peaceful and present. Whether I am standing on a street or in an intensive care unit waiting area, or talking about hugs, I am as present as possible. I am there, in the moment, in a very real way. The more present I am, the more I am able to let go of my expectations and desires of how I want things to unfold, allowing them to occur naturally. It is over a great deal of time that this has happened and that I have opened myself up to it.

When I first started offering hugs, I had expectations of what I wanted to happen. I wanted others to take me up on my offer or to recognize me for doing something so special in the world. I was looking outside of myself to have something happen, in order to feel good inside of myself. Of course, I always have known—and now, more deeply understand—that the joy does not lie outside of me, ever. As a result, my offering of hugs to others has now brought a deep peace and knowing to me that I had not experienced before. As I allow the unfolding of it to happen on its own, beautiful circumstances come to me. I understand that I need not plan it out or think about it, but just allow it to be. Allowance holds within it great power, beauty, and love.

And the most beautiful part is this is just the beginning of an amazing journey that has no end.

Epilogue

This story of mine will never be over. It will continue to expand, evolve, and grow, a metamorphosis. Every time I step onto a sidewalk and put on my Free Hugs sign, I learn a new lesson. Sometimes about surrender. Sometimes about loving others as they are. Sometimes about how to be in the present moment. All these lessons will continue to be essential for my growth as a human being and for my realization as a spiritual being.

It is rare now that a week goes by that I am not out hugging people in some location. It has not only become something that I thoroughly enjoy; it has become my practice, my mantra, my way of offering thanks and receiving so much in return.

To all of you whom I have hugged, loved, or seen, and for those of you reading this without that experience so far, *thank you*. You continue to inspire me and fan the flames of my soul, and I am forever grateful.

Until we meet in person, please remember:

Hug some one.

My Book Selections

These are the books on my shelf at home and on my Kindle for travel that I rely on the most. I have reread each of them, some multiple times. I hope that you enjoy them already or will come to enjoy them.

The Power of Now by Eckhart Tolle

The New Earth by Eckhart Tolle

The Four Agreements by don Miguel Ruiz

A Course in Miracles

Awaken Your Inner Fire by HeatherAsh Amara

The Voice of Knowledge by don Miguel Ruiz

The Fifth Agreement by don Miguel Ruiz

The Mastery of Love by don Miguel Ruiz

About the Author

Vanessa L. White Fernandes has been a social worker for more than thirty years. She has both a bachelor's and a master's degree in the fields of social work and counseling. She has been a writer most of her life and has maintained a blog for twelve years. This is her first published book. Her family includes her son and her wife, and they live in Northeast Pennsylvania. Her website is www.thehuggingarmy.org. Her Facebook page is "The Hugging Army: An Experience in Connection," and her blog is https://www.vanessaleighsblog.wordpress.com.

Printed in the United States
By Bookmasters